Jasmin Peskoller

The Multicultural Classroom
Learning from Australian First Nations Perspectives

Forschungsschwerpunkt Kulturelle
Begegnungen - Kulturelle Konflikte

Jasmin Peskoller

THE MULTICULTURAL CLASSROOM
Learning from Australian First Nations Perspectives

Bibliografische Information der Deutschen Nationalbibliothek
Die Deutsche Nationalbibliothek verzeichnet diese Publikation in der Deutschen Nationalbibliografie; detaillierte bibliografische Daten sind im Internet über http://dnb.d-nb.de abrufbar.

Bibliographic information published by the Deutsche Nationalbibliothek
Die Deutsche Nationalbibliothek lists this publication in the Deutsche Nationalbibliografie; detailed bibliographic data are available in the Internet at http://dnb.d-nb.de.

Gefördert durch den Forschungsschwerpunkt ‚Kulturelle Begegnungen – Kulturelle Konflikte' der Leopold-Franzens-Universität Innsbruck

ISBN-13: 978-3-8382-1587-7
© *ibidem*-Verlag, Stuttgart 2021
Alle Rechte vorbehalten

Das Werk einschließlich aller seiner Teile ist urheberrechtlich geschützt. Jede Verwertung außerhalb der engen Grenzen des Urheberrechtsgesetzes ist ohne Zustimmung des Verlages unzulässig und strafbar. Dies gilt insbesondere für Vervielfältigungen, Übersetzungen, Mikroverfilmungen und elektronische Speicherformen sowie die Einspeicherung und Verarbeitung in elektronischen Systemen.

All rights reserved. No part of this publication may be reproduced, stored in or introduced into a retrieval system, or transmitted, in any form, or by any means (electronic, mechanical, photocopying, recording or otherwise) without the prior written permission of the publisher. Any person who does any unauthorized act in relation to this publication may be liable to criminal prosecution and civil claims for damages.

Printed in the EU

This book acknowledges the past and present Traditional Custodians of the Lands across Australia and pays respect to their Culture and Identity which has been bound up with the Land and Sea for generations.

Education can only be successful if students are met where they are, linguistically and culturally.

Acknowledgments

First and foremost, I would like to express my gratitude to Barbara Hinger, professor of foreign language education at the University of Graz, for her continuous support and for her encouragement to conduct further research in this intriguing field. Moreover, I am thankful for the valuable feedback from Eva Maria Hirzinger-Unterrainer, professor of foreign language education at the University of Innsbruck, in connection with this book.

I am also particularly grateful for the fruitful collaboration with Australian author and linguist Margaret James, who introduced me to her ambitious projects with remote Australian communities and let me use her inspiring language learning materials for my book. Moreover, the research study would not have been possible without the generous support from Prof. Juanita Sherwood, pro-vice-chancellor of Indigenous Engagement at Charles Sturt University. In addition, I would like to thank Larry Hancock, a Gumbaynggirr language teacher in New South Wales, for allowing me to include one of the songs and lyrics he composed in the traditional Indigenous language of Gumbaynggirr in this book.

Naturally, I would like to thank all the dedicated teachers, teaching assistants, principals, and university professors who were willing to share their valuable perspectives, experiences, and time with me and thereby vitally supported the research project.

Finally, a special *cheers* goes to all my mates in Austria, Australia, and other parts of the world for their continuous encouragement and support. I am particularly grateful for the critical eye from my friends and colleagues Alice, Elena, James, Sandra, Magdalena, Theresa, Benny, Theresa, Veronika, Nicola, Kathrin, Grit, Sofie, Alexandria, Fabian, and Lukas in connection with this book.

Without all of these special human beings, this book would have never evolved the way it did.

You are deadly![1]

---

[1] *Deadly* is an expression in Aboriginal English denoting *fantastic* (Arthur 1996).

Muya Wajaarra[2]

Muyalu nyanuum-bigamba ngaanya x3
Let your light come down into me (and fill me up)
Let your breath come down into me (and fill me up)
Let your spirit come down into me (and fill me up)
Let your spirit come down into me (miilarramba ngaanya)
Wajaarra nganyu (miilarramba ngaanya)
Gayirri nganyu (miilarramba ngaanya)

(guitar, sticks)

Giidany nginu jalaawa
Giidany bulaamba jalaawa
Giidany ngujaamba jalaawa
Giidany ngaanyu jalaawa (miilarramba ngaanya)

Ngayan-nginu jalaawa
Ngayan-bulaamba jalaawa
Ngayan ngujaamba jalaawa
Ngayan ngaanyu jalaawa (miilarramba ngaanya)

Muyalu-nyanuum-bigaamba ngaanya (miilarramba ngaanya) x3
Let your light come down into me (miilarramba ngaanya)
Let your breath come down into me (miilarramba ngaanya)
Let your spirit come down into me (miilarramba ngaanya)

Muyalu nyanuum-bigaamba ngaanya (miilarramba ngaanya) x3
miilarramba ngaanya x2

---

[2] Song in the traditional Indigenous language of Gumbaynggirr, a variety spoken in New South Wales; lyrics and English translation by Larry Hancock, Gumbaynggirr language teacher.

Spirit Come Down[3]

Spirit saturate me fully x3
Let your light come down into me (and fill me up)
Let your breath come down into me (and fill me up)
Let your spirit come down into me (and fill me up)
Let your spirit come down into me (fill me)
Come down to earth into me (fill me)
Pour into me (fill me)

(guitar, sticks)

Moon descend into you (one)
Moon descend into you (two)
Moon descend into you (all)
Moon descend into me (fill me)

Sun descend into you (one)
Sun descend into you (two)
Sun descend into you (all)
Sun descend into me (fill me)

Spirit saturate me fully (fill me) x3
Let your light come down into me (fill me)
Let your breath come down into me (fill me)
Let your spirit come down into me (fill me)

Spirit saturate me (fill me) x3
fill me x2

---

[3] Song in the traditional Indigenous language of Gumbaynggirr, a variety spoken in New South Wales; lyrics and English translation by Larry Hancock, Gumbaynggirr language teacher.

Table of Contents

Acknowledgments 7
List of Tables 14
List of Figures 15
List of Abbreviations 16

Preface by *Barbara Hinger* 17

Chapter I: Introduction 19
    1. Background and Relevance 20
    2. Approach and Objectives 22
    3. Structure of the Book 23

Chapter II: Foundations of Multicultural Classrooms 25
    1. Language and Multilingualism 25
    2. Culture and Multiculturalism 29
    3. Teaching and Learning in Multicultural Classrooms 32
        3.1 Perspectives on Diversity in Education 32
        3.2 Implementing Bilingual and Bicultural Approaches.... 35
            3.2.1 *Two-Way Education* 37
            3.2.2 *Immersion Education* 38
        3.3 Education Policies 40

Chapter III: Languages and Cultures in Australia 45
    1. Multilingualism and Multiculturalism 45
    2. The Multicultural Australian Classroom 47
    3. Indigenous Australia 49
        3.1 The Bilingual Context 52
            3.1.1 *The Significance of Indigenous Languages* 54
            3.1.2 *The Significance of the English Language* 56
        3.2 The Bicultural Context 63

Chapter IV: First Nations Education in Australia 67
1. A History of First Nations Education 67
2. Foundations of Indigenous Teaching and Learning 78
   - 2.1 Relationships 79
   - 2.2 Storytelling and Yarning 80
   - 2.3 The Concept of Shame 81
3. Proposed Frameworks and Pedagogies 82
   - 3.1 Eight Ways of Aboriginal Learning 82
   - 3.2 Culturally Nourishing Pedagogy 86
   - 3.3 Culturally Responsive Pedagogy 88
4. Adopted Approaches in Australian Schools 88
   - 4.1 Two-way Schooling 89
     - 4.1.1 *Two-way Bidialectal Education* 90
     - 4.1.2 *Worawa Aboriginal College* 94
   - 4.2 The Stronger Smarter Approach 94
5. Challenges in Indigenous Australian Education 96

Chapter V: Research Study 103
1. Current Research Directions 103
2. Objectives and Design of the Study 112
   - 2.1 Procedure 114
     - 2.1.1 *Constructing the Interview Form* 114
     - 2.1.2 *Transcribing the Interview Data* 115
     - 2.1.3 *Coding the Transcripts* 117
   - 2.2 Sample 118
3. Findings 120
   - 3.1 The Role of Indigenous Languages 120
     - 3.1.1 *Pride vs. Embarrassment* 121
     - 3.1.2 *Recognition of Linguistic Heritage* 122
     - 3.1.3 *Orality of Indigenous Languages* 122
     - 3.1.4 *Code-switching* 123
     - 3.1.5 *Language Concepts and Worldview* 123

	3.2	The Role of Indigenous Cultures 124
		3.2.1 Pride in Culture 125
		3.2.2 Relationship Building 126
		3.2.3 Family and Community Involvement 126
		3.2.4 Home Values and Worldview 127
		3.2.5 Cultural Concepts and Learning Styles 127
	3.3	Frequency Analyses of Language and Culture Categories 128
	3.4	Challenges in Indigenous Education 132
		3.4.1 Historical Burden 133
		3.4.2 Culture-related Differences 133
		3.4.3 Lack of Awareness and Recognition 134
		3.4.4 Systemic Shortcomings in Education 135
		3.4.5 Lack or Stereotypical Inclusion of Culture ... 136
		3.4.6 Socio-economic and Health Parameters 136
	3.5	Frequency Analyses of Challenge Categories 137
	3.6	Incorporating Indigenous Perspectives 140
		3.6.1 The Importance of Incorporating Indigenous Language and Culture 140
		3.6.2 Strategies for Incorporating First Nations Perspectives 142
		3.6.3 Analysis of the Honey Ant Readers Textbooks 144
4.	Summary and Discussion of Findings 154	
	4.1	Summary of Findings 155
	4.2	Discussion of Findings 157
5.	Implications for Teaching Practice 163	

Chapter VI: Conclusion and Outlook 169

Bibliography 173

Appendix: Interview Form 183

List of Tables

Table 1:	A Typology of Bilingual Education	36
Table 2:	Types of Immersion Education	39
Table 3:	Decisive Factors in Immersion Education	39
Table 4:	Stages of Education Policies for Language Minority Groups	42
Table 5:	Indigenous Population in Australia	50
Table 6:	Expressions in AE and their SAE Equivalents	62
Table 7:	Comparison of Indigenous and non-Indigenous Cultural Tendencies	65
Table 8:	Policies Affecting Indigenous Education	71
Table 9:	Conceptual Framework for Learning in the Australian Curriculum	75
Table 10:	Indigenous and non-Indigenous Students' Reading and Numeracy	77
Table 11:	Tendencies in Indigenous and non-Indigenous Learning Practices	79
Table 12:	The Four Pillars of Culturally Nourishing Pedagogy	87
Table 13:	Two-way Bidialectal Education with Practical Outworking	92
Table 14:	Concepts of the *Stronger Smarter Approach*	95
Table 15:	Current Research Directions in First Nations Education	104
Table 16:	Findings from the *Dare to Lead* Project	106
Table 17:	Conventions for Transcriptions	116
Table 18:	Transcribed and Omitted Information	116
Table 19:	Duration of Interviews	117
Table 20:	Characteristics of the Sample	119

List of Figures

Figure 1:	Differentiation of the Language Concept	26
Figure 2:	Forms of Bilingualism	28
Figure 3:	Aims of Bilingual Education Models	35
Figure 4:	Aboriginal Languages and Nations in NSW and ACT	55
Figure 5:	The Continuum of Aboriginal English	59
Figure 6:	Intercultural Understanding in the Australian Curriculum	73
Figure 7:	Eight Ways of Aboriginal Learning	83
Figure 8:	The Boomerang Matrix	85
Figure 9:	The Framework of Culturally Nourishing Pedagogy	86
Figure 10:	Strategies of the *Stronger Smarter Approach*	96
Figure 11:	Research Questions	113
Figure 12:	Perspectives represented by the Sample	119
Figure 13:	Language-related Factors Identified in the Interview Data	120
Figure 14:	Culture-related Factors Identified in the Interview Data	125
Figure 15:	Frequency of Codes: Language and Culture	129
Figure 16:	Code-Matrix-Browser: Language and Culture	131
Figure 17:	Challenges Identified in the Interview Data	132
Figure 18:	Frequency of Codes: Challenges	137
Figure 19:	Code-Matrix-Browser: Challenges	139
Figure 20:	Importance of Incorporating Linguistic Backgrounds	140
Figure 21:	Importance of Incorporating Cultural Backgrounds	141
Figure 22:	Storytelling Methodology in the HARs	147
Figure 23:	Culturally Relevant Contents in the HARs	148
Figure 24:	Recognition of AE in the HARs	149
Figure 25:	Concept of Orality in the HARs	150
Figure 26:	Songs in the HARs	152
Figure 27:	Rhymes in the HARs	152

List of Abbreviations

ACARA	Australian Curriculum, Assessment and Reporting Authority
ACT	Australian Capital Territory
AE	Aboriginal English
ATSI	Aboriginal and Torres Strait Islander People
CEFR	Common European Framework of Reference for Languages
EFL	English as a Foreign Language
ESL	English as a Second Language
HARs	Honey Ant Readers
IA	Indigenous Australian
NAPLAN	National Assessment Program—Literacy and Numeracy
NSW	New South Wales
NT	Northern Territory
QLD	Queensland
SA	South Australia
SAE	Standard Australian English
TAS	Tasmania
VIC	Victoria
WA	Western Australia

Preface

Seeing one of your students proceed in research after having finished their diploma studies is always a pleasure for a supervisor. In her very first course on foreign language education at the University of Innsbruck, Jasmin was one of my students. Her interest in the various topics presented and discussed in the sessions was immediately observable. During her studies, Jasmin enrolled as an exchange student at the University of Technology, Sydney, where she was awarded a study abroad excellence grant. Impressed by the cultural richness and Indigenous heritage, Jasmin started to plan a research project investigating the interface of education and Indigenous cultures in Australia and decided to apply for an international research funding offered by the University of Innsbruck. Her application being successful, Jasmin returned to Australia to carry out her diploma thesis project on the very topic she presents in this book. Learning from Australians First Nations Perspectives is what Jasmin embraced to do in her exploratory, small-scale interview study with 11 experts in the field of Australian First Nations education whilst also glancing at two volumes of the *Honey Ant Readers* textbook series put forward by Margaret James.

All in all, it takes quite some courage and curiousness to open up to a culturally diverse and pretty different background to one's own. Jasmin successfully stepped into that endeavor due to her goal-orientation as well as her outstandingly open-hearted and communicative qualities which made her pursue a challenging target in a self-paced way. Hence, Jasmin's contribution offers valuable insights and fresh perspectives, strengthens research on Australian First Nations education and raises the issue of multilingual classrooms in an increasingly diverse world.

Finally, I'd like to acknowledge the Traditional Owners of the land on which Jasmin carried out her research. I would also like to pay my respect to their Elders past and present and extend that respect to all Aboriginal and Torres Strait Islander peoples today.

Barbara Hinger
July 2021, Graz, Austria

Chapter I

Introduction

> Education is the most powerful weapon which you can use to change the world.
>
> **Nelson Mandela, in a speech at Madison Park High School, Boston, 23 June 1990 (Ratcliffe 2018)**

Nelson Mandela, one of the most distinguished activists, politicians, and revolutionaries for freedom and equality, expresses the effectiveness and fundamental importance of education in the above quote. As a result of the possibility and responsibility of equipping learners with the necessary knowledge, skills, and attitudes for citizenship, and thus preparing them for participation in a global society, educators are accorded a highly significant role. As multilingualism and multiculturalism constitute increasing realities in societies and classrooms across the globe, it is of particular importance for educators to learn about the factors connected to students' home language and culture that can facilitate or impede their learning and to revise teaching materials and methodology accordingly.

Due to my role as a teacher and teacher educator, the aspect of cultural diversity and student heterogeneity inside classrooms has always been of particular interest and relevance to me, something my work with refugee students as well as my research project in Australia certainly amplified. Originally, my genuine interest in approaches to teaching and learning in multicultural classrooms with a specific focus on First Nations education was kindled through a case study I conducted at an Aboriginal school. I explored their methodologies as an assignment during my study-abroad semester in Sydney. Later, my work in a transition class for juvenile refugee students in Austria reinforced this interest and generated the desire to provide the necessary, evidence-based underpinnings for a more equitable education system and effective classroom practice through research. This book presents a research project which investigated the inclusion of First Nations perspectives in the multicultural Australian school setting.

Prior to the composition of this book, which is based on a Diploma Thesis at the University of Innsbruck, Austria, some insights into the research findings were presented at international conferences and published as proceedings papers (refer to Peskoller [2019] for a publication in English and Peskoller [2018] for a publication in German). However, this book presents and discusses the research project in its entirety and grants full access to the data obtained from the Australian educational context.

The inclusive term *Indigenous Australian* is used throughout the book to pay respect to people past and present who identify as Aboriginal and/or Torres Strait Islander, the two Indigenous groups in Australia. Moreover, as "[o]ne of the great mythologies of Indigenous education and educational research is that there is one singular, homogeneous entity of the 'Indigenous Community'" (Philips & Luke 2017, 960), the denotation *First Nations* Australians proves beneficial as a way of acknowledging them as the traditional inhabitants, owners, and custodians of the land and sea, while simultaneously alluding to the great diversity within Indigenous Australia. If not specifically annotated, the term *Aboriginal* is also used with the same inclusive and appreciative reference.

In this introductory chapter, the background and relevance of the study is discussed and its approach and objectives are briefly illustrated through a presentation of the underlying research questions. Finally, a structure of the book is provided.

1. Background and Relevance

In this day and age, numerous individuals with increasingly diverse linguistic and cultural backgrounds meet and negotiate meaning on a regular basis. As the scope of multilingualism and multiculturalism within societies is increasing on a global scale, schools have developed into meeting places for a growing number of languages and cultures (Bierwirth et al. 2017). Consequently, discussions on the significance of including a variety of perspectives in classroom discourse and the imperative of ridding the latter of a prevailing monocultural straitjacket have emerged. Against the backdrop of these changing realities, authors have advocated for revisions and adaptions of current teaching methodologies and classroom materials in order to do greater justice to an increasingly diverse student population.

While certain areas of the world might have only recently experienced this global phenomenon, Australia's society has always been characterized by multiculturalism. This reality derives from the fact that the country was initially inhabited by the already multilingual and multicultural First Nations peoples, constituting the oldest living culture in the world (ACARA, n.d.b), and evolved into an immigrant nation as a result of colonialization (Ellis, Gogolin & Clyne 2010, 441). More specifically, before European settlement started in 1788, at least 200 Indigenous languages were spoken throughout the country. Since many of these had regional dialects and varieties, an estimated 500 ways of speaking existed in Indigenous Australia. Unfortunately, due to processes of colonialization and atrocious policies of assimilation, fewer than 80 of these varieties have survived into the 21st century (Arthur 1996, 1). In 1978, Australia officially declared itself to be a multicultural nation (Liddicoat 2009, 190).

Today, First Nations Australians find themselves living a multilingual and multicultural life. On the one hand, traditional ways of knowing, being, and doing are still important for the maintenance of a strong sense of identity. On the other hand, showing an understanding of the dominant, non-Indigenous culture and being proficient English language speakers are essential requirements for Indigenous Australians to achieve success in society. For many Indigenous students, school education constitutes the main medium for becoming acquainted with the non-Indigenous language and culture.

As the development of high-quality materials and valuable approaches to teaching and learning constitutes a core endeavor in educational research, and due to the fact that multilingualism and multiculturalism have evolved into central characteristics of global societies and classrooms, this research study aims at providing insights from the learning context of Indigenous students in Australia, a country acclaimed for its linguistic and cultural diversity. Specifically, the project investigates factors connected with Indigenous Australian students' linguistic and cultural backgrounds that are essential for their learning in school, identifies related challenges for everyday schooling, and sheds light on educational approaches which experienced educators in the field propose for multicultural classrooms. At the interface of the increasingly multicultural nature of classrooms across the globe and the insights from First Nations education in Australia, the findings should be relevant to all educators striving to support their diverse students' learning as best as possible.

2. Approach and Objectives

The research project aimed at identifying language- and culture-related factors that experienced educators in Indigenous education perceive as relevant for Indigenous learners. The study also attempted to identify existing challenges in First Nations education and to collect effective strategies for considering First Nations perspectives in teaching materials and methodology. In order to obtain the desired insights, semi-guided interviews were conducted with experts in Indigenous education. Specifically, the questions guiding the qualitative study read as follows:

- Which language- and culture-related factors do experienced educators perceive to impact Indigenous Australian students' learning at school?
- Which challenges exist in teaching and learning with Indigenous Australian students and how can Indigenous perspectives be incorporated in teaching materials and methodology?

Multiple perspectives were collated in the study as Indigenous and non-Indigenous teachers, teaching assistants, principals, and university lecturers shared their perspectives and experiences. Substantiated insights into the multilingual and multicultural learning context of

Australian First Nations students were obtained. Based on the findings from this explorative study focusing on Indigenous Australia, strategies for teaching practice in multicultural classrooms in Australia and beyond can be derived. Hence, the outcomes and implications of the study should provide assistance to all educators in a day and age where linguistic and cultural diversity has become the global norm.

3. Structure of the Book

The book consists of six chapters:

Chapter 1: Introduction

An overview of the background and relevance as well as the objectives of the research study are given.

Chapter 2: Foundations of Multicultural Classrooms

The fundamental concepts of language, multilingualism, culture, and multiculturalism are defined. Subsequently, the focus shifts to multicultural classrooms starting with a discussion on perspectives on diversity in education. Then, approaches to teaching and learning in multicultural classrooms are presented and relevant education policies are outlined.

Chapter 3: Languages and Cultures in Australia

The concepts of multilingualism and multiculturalism are discussed in the context of Australia. Focusing on its First Nations, the significance of languages in Indigenous Australia is highlighted, examining both traditional Indigenous languages and varieties of English. Finally, Indigenous Australians' ways of knowing, being, and doing are introduced and the multicultural realities of First Nations Australians are highlighted.

Chapter 4: First Nations Education in Australia

A brief historical account of First Nations education including relevant policy documents is provided and cultural foundations of Indigenous approaches to teaching and learning are explored. Moreover, proposed frameworks for Indigenous education as well as adopted approaches at specific schools in Australia are presented. Lastly, selected challenges in the field are discussed.

Chapter 5: Research Study

After a discussion of current research dimensions in First Nations education, the design and objectives of the empirical study are outlined by illustrating its underlying research questions and design. Subsequently, the findings of the qualitative research study are presented, analyzed, and interpreted. Finally, the results are discussed and implications for teaching practice in multicultural classrooms are derived.

Chapter 6: Conclusion and Outlook

The last chapter contains a concise review of the study conducted and suggests potential directions for further research in the field.

Chapter II

Foundations of Multicultural Classrooms

Since "we all see the world differently, our context and experiences are divergent, and the way we explore language is again distinctive" (Power et al. 2015, 4), this chapter defines the key concepts of language and multilingualism as well as culture and multiculturalism. Having established this fundamental terminology, perspectives on diversity in education are discussed and select approaches to teaching and learning in multicultural classrooms are explored. In conclusion, education policies affecting multicultural classrooms are addressed.

1. Language and Multilingualism

Fundamentally, languages constitute systems of interrelated signs used for the purpose of communication (Edmondson and House 2011, 7-8) and can thus be described as "fluid codes framed within social practices" (García 2009, 49). Concurrently, Eades (2013, 57) states that "language is much more than the reflection or expression of society and culture; it is a dynamic and creative instrument of social action". Investigating its symbolic nature, Kramsch (2009, 7) highlights that language use "mediates our existence through symbolic forms that are conventional and represent objective realities" and that "construct subjective realities such as perceptions, emotions, attitudes, and values."

In relation to the concept of language, a distinction between dialect and accent also needs to be provided at this stage. Endorsing the existence of a continuum between language varieties and dialects depending on regional, societal, political, and cultural leverages, sociolinguist Trudgill (2000, 5) provides the following definitions:

> The term *dialect* refers, strictly speaking, to differences between kinds of language which are differences of vocabulary and grammar as well as pronunciation. The term accent, on the other hand, refers solely to differences of pronunciation, and it is often important to distinguish clearly between the two.

As the concept includes both standard and non-standard varieties of a language, Standard English should itself be regarded as a dialect of English due to its distinct grammatical and lexical features. In this context, authors have complained that standard varieties are often considered the only proper way to speak and they have accentuated the fact that a society's values and structures are displayed in the attitudes towards non-standard varieties (e.g. Trudgill 2000, 5–9). This aspect alludes to the slow recognition of Aboriginal English as a distinct dialect of Standard Australian English (SAE), which is explored in Chapter III.3.1.

In the context of language teaching and learning, a differentiation between home, second, and foreign languages is essential. The following figure should assist readers in understanding this fundamental terminology.

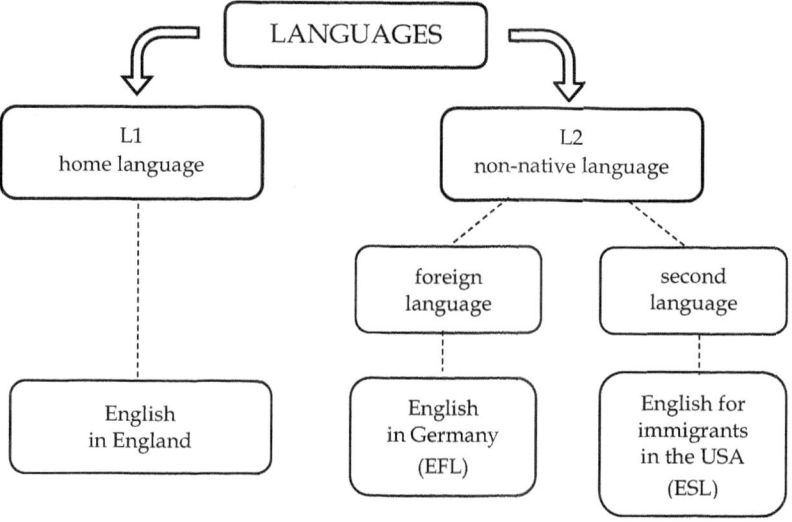

Figure 1: Differentiation of the Language Concept[4]

In order to differentiate between the two non-native languages in Figure 1, the function and purpose of the language are decisive factors. Putting the focus on English language teaching, the acronyms *ESL* (English as a Second Language) and *EFL* (English as a Foreign

---

[4] Modified from Edmondson & House 2011, 8.

Language) exemplify the two concepts. In ESL contexts, learners might still practice their L1 at home but need English as the means of communication in everyday life, as is for instance the case in Australia, Canada or the UK. The term EFL, on the contrary, pertains to contexts in which English does not play an essential role within society, as it is not necessarily required for communicative purposes or in educational settings due to other dominant languages. It is necessary to differentiate between ESL and EFL contexts, since syllabuses, classroom pedagogies and education policies usually display considerable differences (Carter & Nunan 2001, 2).

The focus is now transferred to the coexistence of two or more language varieties within one speech community or country, which is generally denoted bi- or multilingualism, respectively. In simple terms, bilinguals "use two or more languages (or dialects) in their everyday lives" (Grosjean 2010, 4). Conversely, other authors have adopted the concept of multilingualism to "describe the use of three or more languages by an individual or within a society" (Baker & Wright 2017, 431). The *Common European Framework of Reference for Languages* (CEFR) defines multilingualism rather broadly as "the knowledge of a number of languages, or the co-existence of different languages in a given society" (Council of Europe 2001, 4). In addition, *bidialectalism* has been used to describe the "phenomenon whereby someone can communicate in more than two dialects of the same language" (Carter & Nunan 2001, 94) and can be regarded as one form of bilingualism. Finally, the concept of *plurilingualism* refers to an individual's totality of linguistic resources in the CEFR (Fäcke & Meißner 2019, 2).[5]

Generally, different manifestations of bilingualism have been identified in the field. For instance, along with other linguists, Brown (2007) makes use of the expressions *subtractive* and *additive* bilingualism to imply the respective status and effect of the home language in and on the processes of learning a new language. In this sense, an L1 "is referred to as subtractive if it is considered to be detrimental to the learning of a second language" whereas "[a]dditive bilingualism

---

5   This book makes use of the terms *multilingualism* and *multilingual* to refer to the totality of an individual's or society's linguistic resources. *Bilingualism* and *bilingual* is used with the same inclusive reference.

is found where the home language is held in prestige by the community or society" (Brown 2007, 139). In this regard, García (2009, 73) addresses the deliberate encouragement that students abandon their home language in favor of the majority language in monolingual schools, thereby ensuring a subsequent monolingual generation. She identifies the treatment of Indigenous children in schools all over the world as possibly the strongest driver for subtractive bilingualism leading to the vast reduction in the number of Indigenous languages. In addition to subtractive and additive bilingualism, García (2009, 73–74) also differentiates between *recursive* and *dynamic* bilingualism in her work. As such, efforts made to revitalize traditional Indigenous languages frequently re-introduce them by assigning them new functions or contexts of use. As speakers move back and forth between different varieties depending on the setting, this form is termed recursive bilingualism. Furthermore, due to globalization and the resulting linguistic complexity in the 21st century, bilingualism and language practices constantly need to adjust to an ever-changing world of multilingual communication, hence reveal highly dynamic features. García illustrates these four types of bilingualism in the following manner (Figure 2):

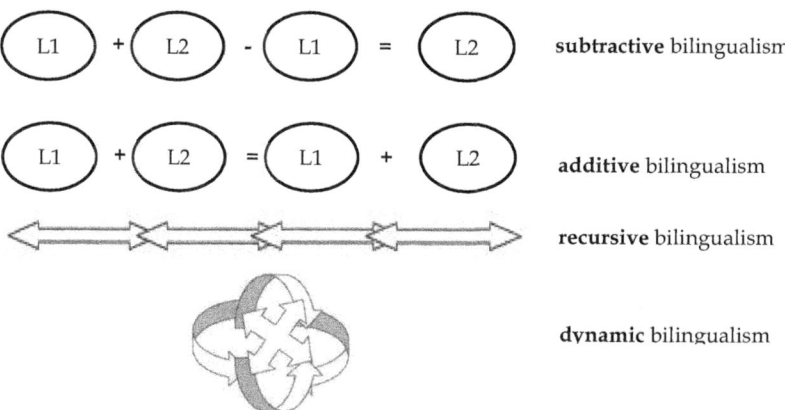

Figure 2: Forms of Bilingualism[6]

---

[6] Data and Images retrieved from García 2009, 72–74.

García's conceptualization of dynamic bilingualism is also apparent in the CEFR, which outlines the following:

> [A]s an individual person's experience of language in its cultural contexts expands [...], he or she does not keep these languages and cultures in strictly separated mental compartments, but rather builds up a communicative competence to which all knowledge and experience of language contributes and in which languages interrelate and interact. (Council of Europe 2001, 4)

Investigating bilingual speakers' usage of different language varieties, a concept of particular relevance is *code-switching*. This involves "the alternate use of two languages, that is, the speaker makes a complete shift to another language [...] and then reverts back to the base language" (Grosjean 2010, 51–52). The term can be used to refer to changes at word, phrase or sentence level in a conversation (Baker 2011, 107). There are different reasons for bilinguals to activate their distinct language systems in this way. First and foremost, there might be a more suitable expression for a certain idea in one language that "adds a little something that is more precise than trying to find an equivalent element in the base language" (Grosjean 2010, 53). Other motives for code-switching include filling a linguistic requirement, identifying with a group or demonstrating one's expertise (Grosjean 2010, 54–55).

According to the CEFR, "[l]anguage is not only a major aspect of culture, but also a means of access to cultural manifestations" (Council of Europe 2001, 6). Hence, the next section defines and discusses the concepts of culture and multiculturalism.

2. Culture and Multiculturalism[7]

Since it is "a far-reaching dynamic concept and an elaborate, everchanging phenomenon" (Wintergerst & McVeigh 2011, 3) an abundance of understandings and definitions of the concept of culture exists. Despite it being one of the most frequently used expressions in the social sciences and humanities, culture is also one of the most

---

[7] Within the scope of this book, an exhaustive presentation of the concept of culture cannot be given. Therefore, an overview of select discussions in the field, and the definition of culture underpinning this research study, is provided.

underdetermined concepts in everyday language use, connoting different phenomena in different contexts and fields of research (Surkamp 2017, 179). Accordingly, Baker (2015, 46) elucidates that "our definitions of culture will always be partial and open to revision and change." Despite the complexity of the field, this chapter includes and discusses select efforts at a definition of both culture and multiculturalism and illustrates the understanding of culture underpinning the study.

To start with, Brown (2007, 132) outlines that "[c]ulture is a way of life. It is the context within which we exist, think, feel, and relate to others." In contrast, Hollins (2015, 20) regards culture as emerging from people's experience and acquired understanding "about how to live together as a community, how to interact with the physical environment, and knowledge or beliefs about their relationships or positions within the universe." Adopting a comparative intercultural perspective, Hofstede and McCrae frame their operating definition of culture as

> [t]he collective programming of the mind that distinguishes one group or category of people from another. This stresses that culture is (a) a collective, not individual, attribute; (b) not directly visible but manifested in behaviors; and (c) common to some but not all people. (Hofstede & McCrae 2004, 58)

This approach exhibits similarities to the two central meanings of culture identified by Throsby (2001). On the one hand, culture is used to "describe attitudes, beliefs, mores, customs, values and practices which are common to or shared by any group." This group "may be defined in terms of politics, geography, religion, ethnicity or some other characteristic" (Throsby 2001, 4) ensuring a sense of identity. On the other hand, culture also "has a more functional orientation, denoting certain activities that are undertaken by people, and the products of those activities, which have to do with the intellectual, moral and artistic aspects of human life" (ibid., 4). In relation to these perspectives, Baker and Wright (2017, 426) define culture as "the set of shared meanings, beliefs, attitudes, customs, everyday behavior and social understandings of a particular group, community or society."

What can be perceived based on these preliminary elaborations is the great diversity of definitions of the concept of culture, which virtually unanimously appear to involve processes of grouping people together according to seemingly shared features and identifying dimensions that distinguish them from others (Dockery 2010, 318). While such approaches may provide comprehensible outlines of the concept, they have been criticized for adopting a simplified, static, and homogeneous understanding of culture, which, in light of the globally increasing scope of diversity in societies and classrooms, has been deemed inappropriate.

On the contrary, as "culture is constantly changing and adapting" (Yunkaporta 2020, 61), authors have advocated for the adoption of an understanding of culture as a complex and dynamic entity including a "multiple, fragmented and hybrid nature of identity" (Baker 2015, 111). In this context, Kramsch (2009, 225–226) pleads for a movement towards a late modernist approach, which abandons a focus on nations and borders, and regards culture as a "dynamic process, constructed and reconstructed in various ways by individuals engaged in struggles for symbolic meaning and for the control of identities, subjectivities and interpretations of history." Based on this understanding, Ladson-Billings (2017, 143) also outlines that

> it is important to emphasize the dynamic and fluid nature of culture that is much more than lists of "central tendencies" or worse, "cultural stereotypes." From an anthropological perspective, culture encompasses worldview, thought patterns, epistemological stances, ethics, and ways of being along with the tangible and readily identifiable components.

Thus, Aboriginal scholar Yunkaporta (2020, 242) concludes that it is "the cultural lens that we carry everywhere with us. […] Your culture is not what your hands touch or make — it's what moves your hands."

As with the criticism raised in connection with the concept of culture, the definitions of bi- or multiculturalism reveal similar predicaments due to the simplifying undertone that afflicts many of them. In the *Encyclopaedia of Bilingual Education*, for instance, the concept of biculturalism is defined as

> the ability to effectively navigate day-to-day life in two different social groups and to do so with the anticipated result of being accepted by the cultural group that is not one's own. […] [The term] refers to the necessary knowledge, skills, and beliefs that individuals can access to participate within their own and another cultural group. (Smith 2008, 65)

Similarly, Baker and Wright (2017, 431) have recently defined multiculturalism as "[a]dopting the cultural practices associated with more than one cultural or ethnic group." In this context, Australian linguist Eades (2013) relates the term biculturalism to the previously discussed concept of multilingualism claiming that "[m]any people are bicultural, having the ability to participate in two or more sociocultural groups — just as bilingual people can speak two or more languages, and bidialectal people can speak two or more dialects" (Eades 2013, 13).

In summary, while various definitions of the concept of culture have been suggested, this book regards culture as an open, complex, dynamic, and highly individual construct. Based on this late modernist understanding (Kramsch 2009), the term *multicultural* is used to describe classroom settings which are characterized by increasingly diverse ways of knowing, being, and doing. In addition, the terms *bicultural* as well as the plural derivative *cultures* are occasionally used with the same inclusive reference in order to accentuate the pluralistic, heterogeneous, and dynamic nature of culture and to emphasize the cultural diversity existing within Indigenous Australia.

3. Teaching and Learning in Multicultural Classrooms

Having defined the fundamental terminology related to the field of study, this section discusses perspectives on including learners' various backgrounds in educational settings and subsequently presents a concise sample of existing approaches to teaching and learning. Lastly, education policies relevant for multicultural settings are outlined.

3.1 Perspectives on Diversity in Education

Fundamentally, Australian educationalist Joseph Lo Bianco (2009, 113) accentuates that "[p]erhaps the strongest indicator of the transformed realities of contemporary education in a globalised world is the depth of cultural, racial and linguistic diversity in schools." Adding to this, the American pedagogical theorist Ladson-Billings (2017, 145) establishes that "all students have culture" and emphasizes that "their culture is a valuable, indeed necessary, starting point for learning." On the basis of these clarifications and their significance for educational settings, all classrooms in this global day and age can be regarded as characterized by an increasing diversity, which takes a likewise increasing number of shapes and forms. In connection with diversity in school, dialectologist Yiakoumetti (2012, 1) states the following:

> Research clearly demonstrates that incorporating linguistic diversity into education can lead to social, cultural, pedagogical, cognitive and linguistic advancement. In spite of this evidence, many educational contexts around the world are characterized by an unwillingness to commit to change and a stance that argues for exclusive use of a prescribed standard variety in the classroom.

Referring to this criticism, Dooley (2009, 75) insists on the need for educators to consider that, for learners, "[u]nderstanding what the teacher says or what is written in texts used in class is a key to academic engagement. Yet, for students who are learning the medium of instruction as an additional language, understanding is often elusive." The transition from the spoken to the written word has been identified as an encumbrance for many bilingual students (Windle 2009, 97–98). Apart from linguistic impediments, culture-related obstacles in diverse classroom settings have been identified, lying in the fact that students reveal "a range of abilities and varying degrees of familiarity with the school context in which they find themselves" (Gearon 2009, 210). In other words, students in one classroom might show drastically divergent views on education and might connect different values, expectations, and functions with schooling in general. In summary, Windle (2009, 96) observes that students frequently "tend to devalue their linguistic and cultural resources, rather than seeing them as resources for learning. For many […] students, bilingualism appears to be a burden rather than an advantage in their engagement with school."

As a consequence, Gearon emphasizes the necessity for teachers, especially in the context of foreign language education, to understand the mechanisms and ramifications of certain factors in connection with teaching and learning, and to adapt their strategies accordingly to support both language learning and intercultural learning (2009, 210). Subsequently, Windle (2009, 106–107) illustrates the following modes of behavior required from instructors in culturally and linguistically diverse classrooms. First, teachers need to disregard the common misconception that bilingualism is the primary cause of low academic achievement. Additionally, they need to design effective approaches to teaching and learning while striving to comprehend the individual student's identity and cultural framework. Doing so can help build a solid foundation of mutual understanding and a connection between students and teachers.

Building on Windle's (2009) plea, however, Ladson-Billings (2017, 145) has underscored the predominantly defective understanding of teachers' own backgrounds and identities as an obstacle. Linking this identified shortcoming with the fundamental objectives of education, Watkins et al. (2016, 62) argue the following:

> With schools as important sites in which values and understandings around cultural diversity are formed, it is imperative that teachers possess the necessary professional capacities to assist students in making sense of the multicultural society in which they live ensuring a sense of civic belonging and social inclusion that provide the basis for an equitable and fair polity.

Specifically, Ladson-Billings (2017, 145) argues that learners need to develop a multicultural perspective through schooling which entails that students "broaden their cultural repertoires so that they can operate more easily in a world that is globally interconnected." Therefore, Boon and Lewthwaite (2016, 468) affirm that teaching staff at educational institutions is required to be culturally competent and needs to possess "the knowledge and skills to effectively teach diverse groups of students."

Specifically investigating contexts in which Standard English is the dominant linguistic variety, Ball and Bernhardt (2012, 209) suggest that "[a] first step that schools […] can take is to acknowledge the validity of children's particular English dialect. This acknowledgement can promote children's sense of being capable learners and of belonging in the mainstream school setting." In conclusion, Partington (2003, 42) states,

> School should be a sanctuary from difficulties experienced outside the school and it should be a place where they [students] can be encouraged to succeed and take advantage of opportunities for education and training. For this to happen, however, schools need to change. This change can only occur through more effective education of teachers.

3.2 Implementing Bilingual and Bicultural Approaches

Generally, a variety of definitions and models of bilingual education and a seemingly equally extensive number of ways for classifying and grouping them exist in the field. Fundamentally, Baker (2011) and Grosjean (2010) emphasize the need for a distinction to be made between approaches in which bilingualism is encouraged and those in which a monolingual classroom is targeted (Baker 2011, 207; Grosjean 2010, 230–235). Thus, a distinction can be made between *strong* and *weak* forms of bilingual education, which can be differentiated from monolingual forms of education (Baker & Wright 2017, 198ff.); similarly, García (2009, 146–153) makes use of the terms *monoglossic* and *heteroglossic* for purposes of differentiation. A further distinction relates to the goals of bilingual education. The three most common types of bilingual education and their respective objectives are listed in Figure 3.

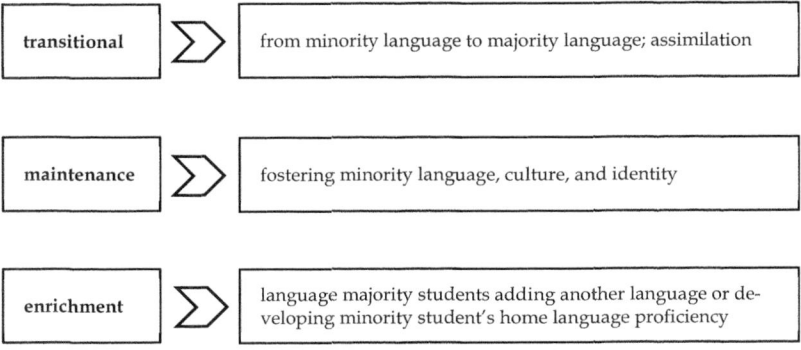

Figure 3: Aims of Bilingual Education Models[8]

Adding to this concise overview of types of bilingual education models, Table 1 depicts an extract from Baker's comprehensive typology of bilingual education to exemplify one way of classifying the various existing approaches to, and sub-branches of, bilingual education.

---

8   Data retrieved from Baker 2011, 207.

Monolingual Forms of Education				
Type of Program	Typical Type of Child	Language of the Classroom	Societal and Educational Aim	Aim in Language Outcome
Mainstreaming/ Submersion	Language Minority	Majority Language	Assimilation	Monolingualism

Weak Forms of Bilingual Education				
Type of Program	Typical Type of Child	Language of the Classroom	Societal and Educational Aim	Aim in Language Outcome
Transitional	Language Minority	Moves from minority to majority language	Assimilation/ Subtractive	Relative Monolingualism
Mainstream (with [Foreign] Language Teaching)	Language Majority	Majority language with second/foreign language lessons	Limited Enrichment	Limited Bilingualism

Strong Forms of Bilingual Education				
Type of Program	Typical Type of Child	Language of the Classroom	Societal and Educational Aim	Aim in Language Outcome
Immersion	Language Majority	Bilingual with initial emphasis on L2	Pluralism and Enrichment	Bilingualism & Biliteracy
Maintenance/ Heritage Language	Language Minority	Bilingual with emphasis on L1	Maintenance, Pluralism and Enrichment	Bilingualism & Biliteracy
Two Way/Dual Language	Mixed Language Minority & Majority	Minority & Majority	Maintenance, Pluralism and Enrichment.	Bilingualism & Biliteracy
Mainstream Bilingual	Language Majority	Two Majority Languages	Maintenance, Pluralism and Enrichment.	Bilingualism

Table 1: A Typology of Bilingual Education[9]

---

[9] Modified from Baker & Wright 2017, 199.

While weak forms of bilingual education include the risk of fostering a subtractive form of bilingualism (see Figure 2), strong forms, on the contrary, encourage additive bilingualism. Connecting the concepts of language and culture, Baker (2011, 249) states that "bilingual education ideally develops a broader enculturation, a more sensitive view of different creeds and cultures" and it "will usually deepen an engagement with the cultures associated with the languages, fostering a sympathetic understanding of differences".

Two approaches that are classified as strong forms of bilingual education in the typology presented in Table 1, immersion education and two-way education, will now be investigated more deeply. In addition, the two-way concept is explored further in connection with contemporary Australian educational discourse in Chapter IV.4.1.

3.2.1 Two-Way Education

Linguist François Grosjean (2010, 239) describes a two-way program as a form of bilingual education "that promotes bilingualism and biliteracy, as well as a very real understanding of the people and cultures involved." Both languages are actively implemented in class and used throughout schooling with students who usually come from one of two main language groups (Grosjean 2010, 239).

In the context of the United States, Baker (2011) outlines that this strong form of bilingual education is typically applied when an almost equal number of minority and majority language speakers exists in one classroom. Baker exemplifies this with a group of learners in which one half speaks Spanish as their home language while the other half speaks English as their L1. Generally, ensuring a language balance in both status and number of speakers in order to prevent one language variety from becoming dominant is paramount in two-way schools (Baker 2011, 222–223).

The major goal of such types of schooling is to foster bilingualism, biliteracy, and biculturalism for all students. In order to achieve this aim, several practices are employed such as assigning both languages equal status, implementing a bilingual school ethos, and making use of bilingual staff members and language minority parents as teacher aides (Baker 2011, 225–226).

3.2.2 Immersion Education

Another possibility for actively acknowledging various linguistic and cultural backgrounds in educational settings is immersion education, which qualifies as a strong form of bilingual education (Baker 2011, 222) (see Table 1). Various scholars have demanded that educational approaches only qualify as immersion education if at least 50% of class time is spent on subject-specific education using a language other than students' L1 for instruction (Surkamp 2017, 134; Tedick, Christian & Fortune 2011, 2).

Generally, Brown (2007) outlines that immersion education is predominantly adopted in additive bilingual contexts in which learners normally share the same home language and show close levels of proficiency in the target language. Frequently, the teachers in immersion education know or even share the students' linguistic or cultural background (Brown 2007, 141). In this regard, García (2009, 149) emphasizes that "[d]espite the immersion of the child in the other language for education, the child's home language is honoured, respected, used throughout the school, and taught right after the immersion period."

Differentiating between programs, Tedick, Christian, and Fortune (2011) name foreign language immersion, bilingual immersion, and Indigenous language immersion as the three major types of immersion education. These as well as their respective characteristics are consolidated in Table 2:

Foreign language immersion programs (one-way)	Bilingual immersion programs (two-way)	Indigenous language immersion programs
• linguistically homogenous students; speaking majority language • additive bilingualism and biliteracy • academic achievement • fostering development of intercultural understanding	• language minority and language majority students • learning each other's languages • additive bilingualism and biliteracy • academic achievement • cross-cultural understanding	• indigenous and increasingly more non-indigenous leaners • revitalize endangered indigenous languages and cultures • can be one- or two-way • additive bilingualism and biliteracy • home identity • academic achievement

Table 2: Types of Immersion Education[10]

Building on this three-fold typology, Baker (2011) suggests a further differentiation be made according to the learners' commencing age and the total amount of immersion time. Table 3 illustrates Baker's approach:

AGE	Early immersion (infant stage)	Middle immersion (approx. ten years)	Late immersion (secondary level)
TIME	Total immersion commences with 100% immersion, reducing to 80% after several years and finishing junior schooling with 50% immersion in the second language per week		Partial immersion comprises 50% immersion in the second language throughout schooling

Table 3: Decisive Factors in Immersion Education[11]

In reference to both Table 2 and Table 3, Surkamp (2017, 134) notes that education systems in multicultural contexts favor two-way immersion programs in which teachers and learners from two language groups work together.

---

[10] Data retrieved from Tedick, Christian & Fortune 2011, 2.
[11] Data retrieved from Baker 2011, 239.

3.3 Education Policies

Building on several of the previously addressed challenges and realities concerning teaching and learning in linguistically and culturally diverse classrooms, different education policies will now be investigated regarding their respective effects on minority language speakers, specifically looking at their situation in schools.[12]

In regards to teaching and learning in multicultural classrooms in a global age, Hornberger (2009, 197) observes that "[e]thnolinguistic diversity and inequality, intercultural communication and contact, and global political and economic interdependence are more than ever acknowledged realities of today's world, and all of them put pressures on our educational systems." Fundamentally, Serra et al. (2018, 33) establish that "the culture of an education system reproduces the culture of a society's dominant classes—in other words, schools are microcosms of societal power structures." Contrasting policy statements and legal documents from designated multilingual and multicultural countries across the globe, it is possible to detect greatly differing levels of importance attributed to them and varying degrees of readiness to implement educational approaches in multicultural classrooms. Hence, Churchill's observation from the 1980s is undoubtedly still valid today:

> [P]olicy making about the education of minorities must cope with an overriding fact: *almost every jurisdiction in the industrialized world is failing adequately to meet the educational needs of a significant number of members of linguistic and cultural minorities.* (Churchill 1986, 8)

Adding to this and to Yiakoumetti's observation in section 3.1., Trudgill (2000, 126) states that the "teaching of minority languages [...] is obviously of benefit to minority-group children, not only in the learning of reading and writing but in other subjects as well." According to Trudgill, doing so would have "an effect of recognizing the child's social and cultural identity and integrity and encourages the development and growth of minority cultures" (ibid., 126). In this sense, Pike (2015, 159–160) identifies the following necessity:

---

[12] A specific analysis of education policies relevant for Indigenous Australian learners can be found in IV.5.

> As majorities can so easily pay scant regard to the wishes of minorities in a democracy, it is vital to educate members of the majority about the perspectives of minorities. […] A focus on understanding and appreciating the differences between the cultural background of minority ethnic groups and the majority should not be eschewed.

Moreover, in connection with modern language education policies and globalization, García, Flores, and Woodley (2012, 72) argue the following:

> As language diversity becomes more complex as a result of globalisation, […] language education policies throughout the world have often become more intolerant of language differences. Thus, more students are increasingly taught in the dominant language of the state without harnessing the linguistic resources they bring.

Also connecting the dimensions of globalization, minority language groups, and education policies, Grosjean (2010, 231) clarifies that

> in areas of the world with minority groups that come from immigration, rare is the country that has a deliberate education policy of allowing minority children to acquire and retain both their home, immigrant language and the majority language, and hence a policy of fostering bilingualism.

In order to receive a better idea of what education policies might or might not undertake in regards to the educational needs of their linguistic and cultural minorities, Churchill's (1986) framework provides an overview of the "six principal policy responses to the educational and language needs of minority groups within the OECD" (May 2012, 18).[13] These are presented in ascending order according to their degree of incorporation and recognition of minority languages in Table 4.

---

[13] OECD is an acronym for the Organization for Economic Co-operation and Development, an international organization which was founded in 1961.

Education Policy	Minority Aspiration
Learning deficit Socially-linked learning deficit Learning deficit from social/cultural differences	Recognition phase
Learning deficit from mother tongue deprivation	Start-up and extension phase
Private use language maintenance	Consolidation and adaption phase
Language Equality	Multilingual co-existence phase

Table 4: Stages of Education Policies for Language Minority Groups[14]

Stage one policies strongly advocate a fast transition to the target language and claim that the use of minority languages is the reason for the educational disadvantage and failure of minority groups. Initial minority aspirations include efforts for the recognition of the existence and specific needs of linguistically and culturally diverse people. At stage two, family and social backgrounds are identified as the main cause for educational detriments for minorities. Thus, programs and projects are enforced to help minority groups adjust to the majority language and culture. Stage three policies recognize that disadvantages for minority groups in education grow from the lack of recognition, acceptance, and a positive attitude towards their languages and cultures. Level four acknowledges that the minority language needs to be supported at least temporarily to facilitate learning and thus incorporates it in the first years of schooling. From this type of transitional bilingualism, minority aspirations might aim at extending minority language programs. At stage five, termed the *private use language maintenance*, minority groups obtain the right to practice their home language and culture in their private lives. A common policy response at this level includes maintenance bilingualism programs in schools, i.e. ongoing schooling in the minority language. Minority aspirations at this stage focus on the

---

[14] Modified from Churchill 1986, 157.

improvement of quality and the incorporation of the minority culture in education. Finally, the minority language is granted official status and autonomy at the *language equality* stage. The latter encompasses an allocation of language programs in several public institutions over which minority groups obtain full control and which they organize and is thus termed the *multilingual co-existence phase* (May 2012, 19–31).

Linking education policies with multilingual education and First Nations perspectives, Hornberger (2009, 197) expresses a "deep conviction that multilingual education constitutes a wide and welcoming educational doorway toward peaceful coexistence of peoples and especially restoration and empowerment of those who have been historically oppressed." Thus, proceeding from an Indigenous perspective, Hornberger proposes ten certainties about multilingual education policy and practice which are relevant for any classroom at a global age (Hornberger 2009, 197):

- National multilingual language education policy opens up ideological and implementational spaces for multilingual education.
- Local actors may open up — or close down — agentive spaces for multilingual education as they implement, interpret and perhaps resist policy initiatives.
- Ecological language policies take into account the power relations among languages and promote multilingual uses in all societal domains.
- Models of multilingual education instantiate linguistic and sociocultural histories and goals in each context.
- Language status planning and language corpus planning go hand in hand.
- Communicative modalities encompass more than written and spoken language.
- Classroom practices can foster transfer of language and literacy development alongside receptive-productive, oral-written and L1-L2 dimensions, and across modalities.
- Multilingual education activates voices for reclaiming the local.

- Multilingual education affords choices for reaffirming our own.
- Multilingual education opens spaces for revitalizing the Indigenous.

With these certainties and the revealed potential of multilingual education for Indigenous voices and perspectives in mind, the next chapter focuses on languages and cultures in Australia.

Chapter III

Languages and Cultures in Australia

Building on the theoretical underpinnings from the previous chapter, this section discusses the multilingual and multicultural realities of Australia, placing a major focus on its First Nations. Hence, the wealth of languages and cultures in the country is discussed and the relevance of individual language varieties in Indigenous Australia is outlined.

1. Multilingualism and Multiculturalism

Australia is often linked to concepts of multilingualism and multiculturalism,[15] since the country "began as an English colony and became a major immigrant nation" (Ellis, Gogolin & Clyne 2010, 441). The country's great linguistic and cultural diversity was revealed in the 2016 census data in which 21% of the 23.4 million people living in Australia spoke a language other than English at home. In total, 300 distinct language varieties spoken in Australian homes, aside from English, were identified; the most common ones included Mandarin, Arabic, Cantonese, Vietnamese, Italian, and Greek. Moreover, nearly half of the population indicated having one or both parents born outside Australia and more than a quarter indicated that they were born overseas themselves (Australian Bureau of Statistics 2017a). In addition, roughly 97% of the Australian population are immigrants or descendants of immigrants and the remaining 3% are Indigenous Australians (Malcolm 2018, 7).

Looking at multicultural Australia from a historical and political perspective, the *Galbally Report* constitutes the first official declaration of Australia's great linguistic and cultural diversity to designate it a multicultural country in 1978. In addition to addressing the issue of social affiliation, the document emphasized the need

---

[15] If not stated elsewhere, this book will make use of the terms *bilingualism* and *biculturalism* to also refer to *multilingualism* and *multiculturalism*.

for intercultural understanding to be achieved through improved multilingual resources that constitute the basis for multiculturalism (Liddicoat 2009, 190). Investigating the consistent interplay between Australia's multiculturalism and its national identity, Moran (2011, 2156) observes that "Australia's national identity has shifted from a racially-based white, British Australia, to a diverse, multi-ethnic, and officially multicultural Australia since the 1970s." In addition, the author argues that the concept of multiculturalism does not only convey Australia's treatment of diversity but has also been vital for the emergence of a stronger national identity and the creation of unity (2159–2162). Hence, "Australia is an ethnically diverse nation" (McCandless et al. 2020, 571).

However, Liddicoat (2009) highlights the existence of a monocultural mainstream in multicultural Australia as he argues that there are two types of individuals within Australian society. On the one hand, multicultural beings adhere to their cultural traditions while adapting to the mainstream Australian culture; on the other hand, monocultural people belong to the generalized culture and tolerate other people's multiculturalism. Liddicoat thus argues that Australia's multicultural reality originates from a "co-existence of people belonging to different cultures, with a common cultural reference point in some unproblematised 'Australian' culture" (2009, 191).

After criticizing this one-way nature characterizing Australian society, Liddicoat expands his argument by looking at Australian First Nations. He claims that the abundance of Indigenous Australian languages and cultures has been largely ignored by multicultural policies that have rather targeted a multicultural immigrant society. While policies in the 1970s aimed at national cohesion, the policies from the 1980s and 1990s were marked by a stronger emphasis on economic internationalism. This gave rise to tension within society, as a distinction between economically useful languages and community languages was generated, creating a newfound hierarchy amongst varieties. Furthermore, as issues of language maintenance and revitalization were of utmost importance, Indigenous languages were still looked at separately. This exclusion resulted in an even greater marginalization of Indigenous languages, deeming them "inferior second languages." After the turn of the century, policies started to show a renewed appreciation of both linguistic and cultural diversity. Looking at immigration and citizenship developments, however, a shift towards a homogenized national norm based on the mainstream culture is noticeable (Liddicoat 2009, 190–201). Similarly, Moran (2011, 2167) also states that

> [d]espite the contribution of multicultural policy to the integration of large numbers of ethnically-diverse immigrants since the 1970s, from the mid-2000s Australia's national governments [...] were less willing than in the past to promote the symbolism of multiculturalism, instead emphasizing Australian citizenship.

Reconsidering the dimension of multilingualism, Malcolm (2018, 1) outlines the following:

> For most of its history, the Australian continent has been the domain of languages other than English. In the comparatively short period of about two hundred and thirty years it has been transformed from a land in which some two hundred and fifty indigenous languages prevailed to one in which, overwhelmingly, English has become the dominant language among both immigrant and indigenous populations.

In this regard, Ellis, Gogolin, and Clyne (2010) observe that due to the prevalence of the English language throughout the world, Australians on average are becoming more reluctant to engage in language learning. Consequently, foreign language teachers in school often neglect students' home languages and the advantages of bilingual education. The interface between multilingualism, multiculturalism, and Australian education will be further discussed in the next section.

2. The Multicultural Australian Classroom

Shifting the focus to the educational context, Morisson et al. (2019, 44) declare that "Australian classrooms are becoming increasingly culturally and linguistically diverse." In 2011, Australia published a policy statement, called *The People of Australia,* in which the country's commitment to strengthening its multicultural nature was re-emphasized (Watkins et al. 2016, 47). Moreover, teachers are required by the Australian National Curriculum to foster intercultural understanding in all subjects (Watkins et al. 2016, 54) (see Chapter IV.1).

Despite such efforts at the interface of multilingualism, multiculturalism, and the Australian education system, Harkins (1994) already remarked in the 1990s that "Australian educational thinking has suffered from a conceptual straitjacket of monolingualism that lingers on into our more multicultural times although it is neither useful nor appropriate" (Harkins 1994, 9). In accordance with this accusation, albeit 25 years later, Morisson et al. (2019, 2) observe that "[t]his rich cultural and linguistic diversity contrasts vividly with the staunchly mono-cultural and mono-lingual reality of contemporary Australian schooling." Similarly, Sarra et al. (2018, 34) outline that the education system is "based around the culture of mainstream Australia." Linking this criticism with First Nations perspectives, Ellis et al. (2010, 455–456) highlight that Australia's true monolingual mindset, within its multilingual society, is best revealed when considering the country's unwillingness to harness the benefits of bilingual teaching and learning and its insufficient support for Indigenous languages.

Morisson et al. (2019, 57) identify reasons for these shortcomings as a lack of "confidence and/or expertise to engage with cultural difference in supportive and educationally productive ways." In this regard, the study by Watkins et al. (2016) has shed light on the practical implementations of multicultural education and its core objectives in Australian classrooms. Specifically, the authors conducted a large-scale survey comprising more than 5,000 practicing teachers in public schools in New South Wales (NSW) in order to provide insights into the opinions, challenges, and needs related to multicultural education, operationalized as comprising the following dimensions: Teaching ESL, promoting positive community relations, developing intercultural understanding, teaching a culturally inclusive curriculum, incorporating anti-racism strategies, and teaching refugee students. The study revealed that fewer than half of the participants had received pre-service training in multicultural education with 14.8% indicating that they never received any type of training with regards to multicultural matters. However, a positive trend was observed due to the significantly higher number obtained looking exclusively at data from early-career educators. Additionally, the authors were able to identify two key needs for improved professional training in "teaching a culturally inclusive curriculum" as well as "developing intercultural understanding" and thus advocate for better governmental support in regards to multicultural education both in pre- and in-service teacher training (Watkins et al. 2016, 50–54).

In conclusion, Watkins et al. (2016), among other authors, plead for an adequate training of teachers in order to do proper justice to the increasingly diverse student population in Australia. With a focus on First Nations perspectives in education, this argument is further elaborated in the following sections.

3. Indigenous Australia

As was highlighted in the Introduction, Aboriginal and Torres Strait Islander people (ATSI) constitute the two Indigenous groups in Australia, exhibiting distinct language varieties and cultural traditions. It is essential to acknowledge the great diversity within these two groups, which is why using the denotation *First Nations* is appropriate. Demonstrating a growth of 18.4% between the 2011 and 2016 census counts (Australian Bureau of Statistics 2017b), Table 5 provides insights into Australia's Indigenous population:

state	Aboriginal and Torres Strait Islander People (ATSI)		Total population	ATSI People proportion of total population
	number	%	number	%
New South Wales (NSW)	265,685	33.28%	7,732,858	3.44%
Victoria (VIC)	57,767	7.24%	6,173,172	0.94%
Queensland (QLD)	221,276	27.72%	4,845,152	4.57%
South Australia (SA)	42,265	5.29%	1,712,843	2.47%
Western Australia (WA)	100,512	12.59%	2,555,978	3.93%
Tasmania (TAS)	28,537	3.57%	517,514	5.51%
Northern Territory (NT)	74,546	9.34%	245,678	30.34%
Australian Capital Territory (ACT)	7,513	0.94%	403,104	1.86%
Australia	**798,365**	**100%**	**24,190,907**	**3.3%**

Table 5: Indigenous Population in Australia[16]

As can be seen from the table, 798,365 people identified as being Aboriginal and/or Torres Strait Islander Australians, amounting to 3.3% of the total population. More specifically, with 265,685 individuals equaling 33.28% of the national total, the majority of Indigenous people live in NSW. In contrast, the NT reveals the highest proportion of Indigenous inhabitants when compared to the other states and territories, with 30.34% of the population being Aboriginal or Torres Strait Islander (Australian Bureau of Statistics 2018). In what follows, a brief historical account is given before the present-day realities of First Nations Australians are illustrated.

Before European settlement, Australia had an estimated 300,000 inhabitants who lived together in distinct communities. These communities spoke their own languages yet remained interconnected through kinship (Malcolm 2018, 8–9). At least 200 Indig-

---

[16] Data retrieved from Australian Bureau of Statistics 2018.

enous languages were spoken throughout the country before colonialism and, since many of them had regional dialects, there existed an estimated 500 ways of speaking in Indigenous Australia (Malcolm 2018, 9; Arthur 1996, 1).

Historically, 1788 marks the dawn of colonialism when the first British settlers set foot on Australian territory claiming it to be *terra nullius* (meaning land belonging to no one) (NSW Ministry of Health 2019, 13). These settlers disregarded the fact that the land had already been inhabited by Indigenous peoples for thousands of years. Land was taken away from First Nations Australians without negotiations and communities were forcefully put into missions or reserves where they were rarely allowed to speak their home languages or practice their cultural traditions. Eades (2014, 418) thus accentuates that "Aboriginal people share with other indigenous minorities around the world the legacies of colonial dispossession." Under misleading titles of policies and initiatives such as the *NSW Aborigines Protection Board* Indigenous Australians' lives were controlled by the government (NSW Ministry of Health 2019). As a result, fewer than 80 of the former 500 Indigenous language varieties were maintained into the 21st century (Malcolm 2018, 9; Arthur 1996, 1).

In addition to this disrespectful treatment, thousands of Indigenous children were separated from their families and sent to non-Indigenous training homes and families over a period of more than 50 years in a gruesome endeavor to assimilate Indigenous Australian children to the non-Indigenous, white, European society (NSW Ministry of Health 2019, 12–15). Aboriginal educationalist Yunkaporta (2020, 11) describes this time as follows:

> [T]he horrific process of European occupation resulted in the removal of most of us from our communities of origin, many to reserves and institutions far from home as part of forcible assimilation programmes. Biological genocide was attempted through large-scale efforts to "breed out" dark skin, with the infamous Stolen Generations representing only one part of this policy. For many women, marrying or submitting to settler males so that their children might pass for white was the only way to survive this apocalypse, while waiting for a safer time to return home.

This chapter in Australian history has had a massive impact on the identity and well-being of its Indigenous population. First Nations Australians today are still in the process of trying to recover from this pain inflicted in the past, and the repercussions are still apparent in the greater poverty and number of health issues, as well as in the disparities between First Nations Australians and non-Indigenous students' educational success (NSW Ministry of Health 2019). The circumstances for Indigenous learners in the Australian school system are discussed in Chapter IV.

Moving from this brief historical overview to present-day realities, First Nations Australians today find themselves living a multilingual and multicultural life due to the effects of colonialization. On the one hand, traditional ways of knowing, being, and doing are still of vital importance for the preservation of a strong sense of identity. At the same time, however, showing an understanding of the non-Indigenous culture and being proficient speakers of Standard Australian English are essential requirements for Indigenous Australians to achieve success in society. In sum, "[m]ost Australian Aboriginal children live in a bicultural and bidialectal context. They are exposed […] to the discourse of Australian English and internalise some of its schemas" (Malcolm & Sharifian 2005, 512). The following subchapters explore this bilingual and bicultural context in greater detail.

3.1 The Bilingual Context

As Eades (2013, 62) puts it, "[t]he Aboriginal priority on developing, maintaining and strengthening social relationships is both reflected in, and created by, the way people speak to each other." Making use of the 2016 census data again, and now looking specifically at language, 83% of Indigenous Australians reported speaking only English while 11% still actively use an Indigenous language at home (Australian Bureau of Statistics 2017b). Before discussing the two major language varieties that play a vital role in the lives of Indigenous Australians today, a more detailed historical account of their development is provided first.

As previously mentioned, an estimated 500 varieties of Indigenous languages were spoken before 1788 (Malcolm 2018, 9). Most of these, however, were not maintained into the 21st century, as in less than 300 years the number of traditional languages actively used throughout Australia has dropped below 80. The reasons for this development include the demise of all speakers of one variety, the deliberate discontinuance of passing down languages to younger generations and the forcible removal of people from their land to live together with other communities in settlements or town camps. The latter led to drastic changes in language use and needs, resulting in the emergence of new variations, so-called *pidgins* and *creoles*, for purposes of communication (Arthur 1996, 1). Essentially, a pidgin can be described as a hybrid language originating from regular contact between people using different language varieties. In contrast, the expansion of languages by means of adding grammatical and functional features for purposes of communication is termed *creolization* (Edmondson & House 2011, 8–9). These linguistic developments in Indigenous Australia are further outlined by Harris (2007, 136):

> Colonized by English, many Indigenous languages would die out, but this linguistic invasion would also prompt the rise of contact languages. Gestures would give way to words, words would be joined into jargons and jargons would stabilize into pidgins. Most pidgins would disappear or English-based pidgins would become Aboriginal English without creolizing first. But some would survive, undergoing creolization to become the primary languages of new communities.

Australian society in the late 18th century therefore exhibited two main groups: the English-speaking European community and the Aboriginal community, speaking a variety of languages. The aforementioned emerging pidgin contained vocabulary and linguistic features from both Aboriginal and non-Aboriginal language varieties. This language form spread from South Australia northwards along with the colonizers, a phenomenon which is often referred to as the *traveling frontier*.

Due to the different traditional languages and socio-linguistic contexts in Indigenous Australia, the pidgin was influenced in different ways across the continent and, thus, regional varieties emerged. In the 20th century, the pidgin developed into *Aboriginal*

English (AE), a distinct form and full dialect of Standard Australian English. AE shows significant differences from SAE but is still intelligible to Standard English speakers (Arthur 1996, 1–2).

Eades (2013, 79) additionally observes that this linguistically expanded language variety of AE has not only been used for communicative purposes between Aboriginal and non-Aboriginal people but also between Indigenous communities without a shared traditional language. In summary, Leitner and Malcolm (2007, 7) provide a concise summary of the most significant language developments in Australian history:

- Decline and loss of many traditional Aboriginal languages. Those that have been retained changed dramatically due to contact;
- Rise of Aboriginal language-based *lingua francas*;
- Reduction of Aboriginal multilingualism to a form of bilingualism that includes varieties of English as one of its components;
- Emergence and growth of a specific variety of English: Aboriginal English; and
- A new Australian language habitat that includes Aboriginal languages.

In conclusion, Malcolm (2018, 21) argues that two varieties of Standard English derived from colonization and co-exist in Australia today: Standard Australian English and Aboriginal English. These varieties of English as well as traditional Indigenous languages are of special importance for First Nations Australians. Therefore, these language varieties are outlined and discussed in the upcoming sections.

3.1.1 The Significance of Indigenous Languages

Despite the vast loss in number, Indigenous Australia still reveals an abundance of traditional language varieties spoken by specific groups in specific regions. To visualize this great linguistic diversity, Figure 4 delineates the Indigenous language groups in NSW and the ACT:

Figure 4: Aboriginal Languages and Nations in NSW and ACT[17]

The Aboriginal scholar Williams (2012) identifies the paramount importance of Indigenous languages for fostering Indigenous identity. He identifies a common feature of all Indigenous Australian languages in the fact that they reveal "a lexicon of sound vocabulary, a lexicon of movement vocabulary and a lexicon of image vocabulary. These vocabularies are highly complex, stratified and regulated by spirit law" (Williams 2012, 7). Australian linguist Eades (2013) elaborates on this complexity by outlining that "differences between neighbouring [Aboriginal] languages were often similar to the differences between, say, English and Spanish. And the languages were complex, with the 'easy' ones matching Latin in their complexity" (Eades 2013, 79).

---

[17] © Reconciliation NSW. This map is based on the AIATSIS map of Indigenous Australia, which was produced for a general reading audience. The map is not definitive and is not the only information available which maps language and social groups. See also AUSTLANG (https://collection.aiatsis.gov.au/austlang/search). The information on which the map is based is contested and may not be agreed to by some traditional custodians. The borders between groups are purposefully represented as slightly blurred. They do not claim to be exact.

Williams emphasizes that "these multi-faceted, multi-layered and multi-stratified language forms that we [Indigenous Australians] once all spoke, sung, danced and imaged with fluency remain omnipresent in our spirit memories, even today, even when we have suffered language and culture loss" (2012, 7). In contrast, connecting the ongoing tragedy of language loss with present realities, McKay (2007, 122) observes that the "loss of Indigenous languages continues in Australia as the shift to various varieties of English by speakers continues."

Harkins (1994, 4–5) looks at Indigenous languages in the contexts of education and argues the following:

> Aboriginal languages were, and continue to be, highly valued, and maintenance of them is seen by Aboriginal people as one of the goals of education. English is also highly valued, as an important additional language to serve as a bridge between Aboriginal and non-Aboriginal realities.

3.1.2 The Significance of the English Language

Risager (2018, 193) describes English as "a transnational phenomenon in the sense that its users move around the world and bring their personal forms of English (their linguacultures) with them into new multicultural and multilingual contexts." In the specific context of Australia, the English language can be seen to have

> twofold ownership: on the one hand, as Australian English, it provides a sense of belonging to all who live in Australia because of the way in which it has been moulded to express a distinctively Australian experience; on the other hand, by way of Aboriginal English, it carries a more particular sense of belonging in that it embodies, for Aboriginal and Torres Strait Islander people, a continuing link with their contact experience and their age-old cultures through the distinctive features it has maintained at all levels of linguistic description. (Malcolm 2018, 1)

It is important to note that English is spoken by a large number of Indigenous people in Australia today. "[O]nce a language of foreign imposition, [English] has been adopted by Aboriginal speakers and made their own" (Malcolm 2018, 185). For most of these speakers, "social aspects of the way it is used reflect and help to maintain and create a culture which is Aboriginal and which shows continuities with traditional Aboriginal cultures" (Eades 2013, 64). Aboriginal English is the variety of Standard English that emerged through the contact between settlers and indigenous populations and provides a "pan-Australian means of the expression of their identity" for First Nations people (Malcolm 2018, 1). The substantial work and research provided by linguists Diane Eades and Ian Malcolm has been of vital significance for the recognition of Aboriginal English as a distinct variety and dialect of SAE. Eades (2013, 2) defines AE in the following manner:

> Aboriginal English is the name given to dialectal varieties of English spoken by the majority of Aboriginal people throughout Australia. The recognition since the 1960s of Aboriginal English as a valid, rule-governed dialect of English is one of the most valuable contributions that linguistics has made to Australian society.

Constituting the predominant means of communication for Indigenous Australians today, AE acts as a valuable tool for expressing and transmitting Aboriginal identity (Malcolm 2018, 24; James 2014; 80; Eades 2014, 418). Malcolm nevertheless notes that, despite this adoption of AE by Indigenous Australians, "since many of its speakers are not bidialectal, it needs to be used in public service, legal and educational settings" (Malcolm 2018, 185). Connecting to this plea, Harkins (1994, 32) observes that "Australia has been slow to recognize Aboriginal varieties of English as part of the wealth of our national linguistic heritage." Harkins criticizes the fact that most research on Aboriginal ways of speaking English in the late 20th century focused predominantly on what was lacking, absent or wrong in the Aboriginal varieties of English studied. On the contrary, in her preface to *Bridging Two Worlds: Aboriginal English and Crosscultural Understanding*, Eades claims that AE "is not an imperfect attempt to learn Standard English" but rather "a complex and coherent language system which is the result of the clever use of the resources of English to express Aboriginal conceptual distinctions" (Harkins 1994, foreword).

There are numerous regional varieties of AE that nevertheless reveal great similarities in their structure and associated cultural practices (Harkins 1994, 186). In his work, Arthur (1996) describes the differences in language use between northern and southern parts of Australia as deriving from differing historical dynamics and processes of colonialization: "In Southern Australia, colonialization has been established longest and the proportion of Aboriginal people to non-Aboriginal people is very low" — and also, "there has been the greatest displacement of peoples and the greatest loss of languages and other traditional aspects of life" (Arthur 1996, 3). On the contrary, language retention in the northern parts of Australia has been more successful. Due to this fact, AE is mostly spoken as a second language in northern Australia and differs greatly from the variety of English spoken by Aboriginal Australians in the south (Arthur 1996, 3). In this sense, Malcolm and Truscott (2012, 230) claim that "[l]ike Australian English, Aboriginal English has undergone significant levelling across the continent so that […] its speakers from widely separated areas readily identify with and understand one another."

Linguistic Features of Aboriginal English

AE reflects several semantic and structural characteristics of traditional Indigenous languages, like the lack of certain prepositions, the use of one word to both describe an action and the intention of an action, and the duplication or extension of a word for emphasis (Arthur 1996, 7).

Rather than regarding it as a single dialect, authors refer to AE as a continuum (James 2014; Eades 2014, 2013; Arthur 1996). In addition, Eades (2013, 3) labels varieties of Aboriginal English *light* and *heavy*, depending on their similarity to Standard Australian English. Similarly, Malcolm (2018, 207) argues that "Aboriginal English exists on a continuum, with a greater commonness with Australian English at one end and with creole at the other." Therefore, the continuum of AE can be visualized as follows:

Light variety of Aboriginal English		Heavy variety of Aboriginal English
Only a few expressions different from Standard Australian English		Extremely different from Standard Australian English; ceases to be AE but is a new language

Figure 5: The Continuum of Aboriginal English[18]

In connection with Figure 5, James (2014, 80) outlines that heavy AE is predominantly found in "remote areas where traditional languages are spoken in the home", whereas the light variation is closer to SAE and thus found "in less remote areas where AE is a first language" (James 2014, 80).

Adding to these elaborations, Harkins (1994, 180) contrasts AE with features of pidgins and creoles. She establishes that AE cannot be regarded as a pidgin due to characteristics such as "[i]ts wide range of structures, and the use by its speakers of most of the features of Standard English, in variation with non-standard features." Furthermore, she argues that AE is not a creole either, as most people in her study revealed that they spoke traditional Indigenous languages as their L1. Harkins maintains that due to its distinct composition of both standard and non-standard features of English, and the fact that many of its speakers are fluent standard English speakers as well, AE cannot be conceptualized as a transitional stage either (Harkins 1994, 180). Therefore, Aboriginal English is best described as a "perfectly adaptable, rule-governed language" (Eades 2013, 61) in its own right.

Functional Features of Aboriginal English

Aboriginal English provides its speakers ways to express Indigenous cultural concepts and meanings through its characteristics

---

[18] Data retrieved from Arthur 1996, 3; Eades 2013, 3; Malcolm 2018, 29.

and structure. In this manner, English can be spoken and regarded as an Aboriginal language, as suggested by Harkins (1994, 184). Despite the fact that AE, like traditional Indigenous languages, is still predominantly an oral language, efforts have been made to include it in books and newspapers in order to make it accessible to a wider reading public (Arthur 1996, 4).

Generally, the ways in which people throughout Australia use AE vary greatly. Some people might speak it as a second language to interact with members of other communities or with non-Aboriginal Australians. Others, however, might speak AE as their home language and use it in every situation of their everyday life. Then again, speakers might code-switch and choose the most appropriate kind of English according to the context. For example, some may speak AE at home and SAE at work with non-Aboriginal people (Arthur 1996, 3). Referring to learners in remote Indigenous communities, James (2014, 79) calls AE the "language of the playground."

Finally, Harkins (1994) identifies two main purposes for Indigenous Australians to use English when communicating with non-Indigenous speakers. First, they use it "to get knowledge, information and things of value from the non-Aboriginal world" and, second, it is used "to communicate to that world what they, as Aboriginal people, think, need, want, and have to say" (Harkins 1994, 5). In her work, Harkins also outlines the willingness and eagerness of many Indigenous people to learn English as they consider it beneficial to communication and mutual understanding without seeing their home languages under threat (Harkins 1994, 17–19).

Aboriginal English and Standard Australian English

This section strives to contrast AE and SAE since "non-Aboriginal people are unaware that English is used in Aboriginal ways, [and] there is considerable communication clash and interracial tension"

(Eades 2013, 55). Seemingly equal expressions in Aboriginal English and Standard Australian English can have greatly divergent meanings and connotations and thus contain the potential to cause communication breakdowns and misunderstandings between Indigenous and non-Indigenous people. Table 6 is a greatly condensed extract from a compilation of vocabulary used in most varieties of AE that should provide an insight into this problematic reality:

Aboriginal English	Standard Australian English
all day	all the time, always, habitually
aunty	an older woman, often wise in traditional knowledge, having status within her community
blackfella	an Aboriginal person
bush tucker	traditional/Aboriginal food
burnt potato	an Aboriginal person who has adopted white Australian attitudes
business	Aboriginal ceremony or ritual
community	A settlement or place where the majority of people is Aboriginal The Aboriginal community as a community of people
country	the tract of land where an Aboriginal person or community belongs, to which they have a responsibility, and from which they can draw spiritual strength; a living entity including the human and non-human, people, culture, spirituality, history, land, waterways, animals, plants, insects, habitats and ecosystems
deadly	great, fantastic, terrific
dreaming	a collection of events beyond living memory which shaped the physical, spiritual and moral world; still manifested in and sustains the present
family	all one's blood relatives
Koori	an Aboriginal person of NSW/VIC
Savvy	to understand
shame	embarrassment; fear; a sense of having transgressed the social and moral code of society, intentionally or unintentionally
uncle	a respectful term of address for an older man
us mob	a connected group
walk	to travel; travel around an area
whitefella	a white person, a European Australian or other person with a similar appearance

Table 6: Expressions in AE and their SAE Equivalents[19]

Aside from lexis, SAE and AE reveal differences in connection with phonology and grammar. In most varieties of AE, double or triple consonant clusters as well as fricatives are rarely used. Additionally, no distinction is made between voiced and unvoiced

---

[19] Data retrieved from Arthur (1996) and Thrope, Burgess & Egan (2021, 56).

phonemes in AE. In regards to grammar, AE exhibits fewer prepositions and a lower use of pronouns and auxiliary verbs than SAE. In contrast, noun phrases are favoured and questions are expressed through a rising intonation (Malcolm 2018; James 2015a).[20]

Contrasting AE with SAE from a cultural viewpoint, Malcolm (2018, 208) denotes SAE as providing an "outsider's perspective" whereas AE serves as an "insider's perspective." Furthermore, he argues that the parallel existence of AE and SAE serves as testimony to a lack of integration of Aboriginal and non-Aboriginal speech communities in Australian society (Malcolm 2018, 23). Malcolm (2018, 22) argues that SAE is considered "the default form for use in education, the law and the administration of public services and competence in SAE is generally agreed to be an expected outcome of education." In this regard, Eades (2014) emphasizes the importance of code-switching abilities for Indigenous learners to move between AE and SAE depending on the context. In this regard, Malcolm (2018, 185) stresses the imperative for AE to "be used in public service, legal and educational settings" since not all speakers of AE are fully bidialectal (Malcolm 2018, 185). This plea connects with one of the many challenges frequently confronting Indigenous learners in Australian classrooms (see Chapter IV.5).

In conclusion, Harkins stresses that "Aboriginal English should be seen, not as a problem, but as part of the linguistic diversity that enriches modern Australian life" (1994, 197).

3.2 The Bicultural Context

Looking at the concept of biculturalism and its meaning and significance for First Nations Australians, linguist Eades (2013, 13) observes that "many bicultural Aboriginal people can switch [...] between Aboriginal ways of interacting and non-Aboriginal ways, depending on the context, the people involved, and the goal to be ac-

---

[20] For a comprehensive account of the characteristics of AE, see Malcolm 2018.

complished." In addition, Eades highlights that even without experience in non-Aboriginal contexts, Indigenous Australians could still be regarded as bicultural since they might have knowledge of two or more distinct Aboriginal ways of knowing, being, and doing (ibid.).

In order to give a brief insight into the character of Aboriginal cultures, Hughes, More and Williams (2004) describe them as neither being defined by numbers nor restricted by time or space. Ancestry is always present in the land and can be interacted with through cultural ceremonies. Creativity, emotions, and social relations are concepts of utmost importance, forming the integral foundation of Aboriginal coexistence (216–220). While the nuclear family is of principal concern, there are wider responsibilities for Aboriginal people including the "rearing of children, the support of the ill or very old people, and the sharing of material resources" (Eades 2013, 58).

Within Indigenous communities, the role of an *Elder* is of special significance. This multifaceted position is held by a person characterized as highly trusted and respected by all members of the community and who embodies the virtues of honesty, integrity, and compassion. Furthermore, an Elder is of unimpeachable character, free of all accusations, and is a mentor and advisor to community members. While showing appreciation and respect for other people's worldviews and value systems, Elders instill a feeling of pride, identity, and self-esteem in Aboriginal people (Sarra 2011, 126–127).

Further concepts vital to Aboriginal identity include avoidance behavior, which refers to aspects like making limited eye contact and assuming specific postures, and the restriction of physical contact or indirectness, which is used to generate more personal space and privacy (Eades 2013, 62–65). Hughes et al. (2004) provide a comprehensive collection and comparison of Aboriginal and non-Aboriginal cultural tendencies (229–249). Some of these dimensions are listed in the following table:

Indigenous	Non-Indigenous
history is timeless	history is quantified and specified
holistic thinking	empirical thinking
fitting into given circumstances	trying to change given circumstances
accepting Aboriginal society	need for change in society
group-oriented	individual-oriented
kinship is important	kinship can be important
spontaneous life style	structured life style
uncritical	critical
listeners	verbalizers/speakers
little eye contact (politeness)	a lot of eye contact (politeness)
indirect questioning	direct questioning
respect for age	respect for youth
giving	saving

Table 7: Comparison of Indigenous and non-Indigenous Cultural Tendencies[21]

As Table 7 illustrates, among other dimensions, "Aboriginal people interact in groups and as members of groups, rather than as individuals" (Malcolm 2018, 113). In this regard, relationships and community constitute essential foundations of knowledge transfer since there "can be no exchange or dialogue until the protocols of establishing relationships have taken place" (Yunkaporta 2020, 149). In relation to sharing information and communicating, three concepts are of utmost relevance in the cultural context of Indigenous Australia: relationship, storytelling, and the concept of shame. As these have particular significance for teaching and learning contexts, they are investigated in further detail in Chapter IV.2.

Like other scholars, Eades (2013) emphasizes that differing cultural practices frequently create misunderstandings between Aboriginal and non-Aboriginal people which can result in the generation and ossification of stereotypes. In this regard, Eades observes that "Aboriginal people often complain that whites are rude, nosey, impatient and ask too many questions. And whites often complain that Aboriginal people are shy, ignorant, slow and uncooperative" (Eades 2013, 74).

---

[21] Modified from Hughes, More, and Williams 2004, 234.

As was illustrated in this chapter, First Nations Australians predominantly live in bilingual and bicultural contexts today. For many Indigenous students, school education is the main medium whereby they become acquainted with non-Indigenous perspectives. In the following chapter, the focus is put on First Nations education in Australia.

Chapter IV

First Nations Education in Australia

On the basis of the previous discussion on teaching and learning in multicultural classrooms, this chapter investigates the specific educational context of Australia by putting a particular focus on the realities and perspectives of its First Nations. Providing a historical account of Indigenous education in Australia, exploring relevant policies at the beginning, an outline of the contemporary situation of Indigenous learners in Australian schools is given. Subsequently, Indigenous approaches to and frameworks for teaching and learning are presented. The chapter concludes with a discussion of contemporary impediments to First Nations education in Australia.

1. A History of First Nations Education

Starting in the late 18th century, "ancestrally perfected ways of learning" (Yunkaporta 2010, 48) in Indigenous Australia "were largely replaced with education systems transplanted from Anglo-European contexts. The 'success' of this education was measured in terms imposed by the colonisers" (Morisson et al. 2019, 1).

Before the 1960s, aspects relating to Aboriginal and Torres Strait Islander affairs constituted responsibilities of the individual states. This led to a great variety of existing education policies affecting Indigenous learners differently across Australia. During that time, First Nations Australians were forced to endure systemic racism and societal discrimination and were frequently denied admission to public schools, as governments did not acknowledge the significance of formal education for Indigenous learners. The only institutions that would accept Indigenous Australian students back then were the Christian missionary schools, which played a significant role in the forcible separation of children from their families as they predominantly aimed at disconnecting Indigenous learners from their cultural heritage. In summary, education was seen as a mechanism to "nullify Aboriginal and Torres Strait Islander culture and identity" (Stone, Walter & Peacock 2017, 93) and was used as an "instrument of assimilation" (Morisson et al. 2019, 7)

In the 1970s, the first national education policies addressing Indigenous Australian matters were introduced, allowing for increased and improved access to education for Indigenous students, though retention and attendance rates were low. Particularly, the establishment of the *Commonwealth Department of Aboriginal Affairs* in 1972 was highly significant for Indigenous Australians' sense of self-determination, since it propelled advancements in First Nations education. For instance, an increased awareness of the various factors impeding educational success for Indigenous learners, such as health problems and poverty, emerged. As a consequence, Aboriginal communities across Australia began to value formal education for their children, even though job prospects in the discriminatory Australian labor market still proved to be rather poor for Indigenous Australians (Zubrick et al. 2006, 39–41). In this regard, Harkins (1994, 4) outlines the meaning of non-Aboriginal education for Aboriginal people:

> Although they have suffered great disadvantage in the non-Aboriginal school system, many Aboriginal people have retained a vision of education as a way for them and their children to get a better understanding of the language and ways of non-Aboriginal Australia, and to acquire knowledge and tools to give them more power over their own lives and enable them to better express their own aspirations and identity.

Sarra (2011) provides a compilation of major reports and policies on Indigenous education, which have emerged since the 1970s. These and further developments significant for Australian First Nations education are outlined in Table 8.

Year	Education Policy / Report	Description
1967	Commonwealth Referendum	Indigenous Australians obtain full citizen rights and are from now on included in the census.
1977	NSW Anti-Discrimination Act	The *NSW Anti-Discrimination Act* made discrimination on the basis of ethnicity, race or gender illegal.
1984	National Policy on Languages	The *National Policy on Languages* was released by the Commonwealth Department of Education to give recognition to Aboriginal languages and AE and to provide funding for more bilingual-bicultural education programs for Aboriginal Australians.
1988	Report of the Aboriginal Education Policy Task Force	The *Aboriginal Education Policy Task Force* was established by the Commonwealth to function as an advisor for Aboriginal education, evaluate the outcomes of the latest research in the field and decide on funding of programs and initiatives.
1990	National Aboriginal and Torres Strait Islander Education Policy (NATSIEP or AEP)	The *NATSIEP*, also called *AEP*, was introduced and committed all Australian governments in three-year arrangements to aim at bringing about equity in education for Indigenous Australians. The 21 long-term national goals can be categorized into four main areas: • Involvement of Aboriginal people in educational decision-making • Equality of access to educational services • Equality of educational participation • Equitable and appropriate education outcomes
1992	Ministerial Council on Education, Employment, Training and Youth Affairs (MCEETYA)	The *MCEETYA* was founded and later released a national review on the effectiveness of the AEP and the education for Aboriginal and Torres Strait Islander Peoples in 1995.
1996	National Strategy for Education of Aboriginal and Torres Strait Islander Peoples 1996–2002	The *MCEETYA* developed a *National Strategy for the Education of Aboriginal and Torres Strait Islander Peoples (1996–2002)* building on the 1995 review. It contained recommendations for reforms in relation to the goals of the *AEP*.

Year	Policy/Document	Description
2000	National Indigenous Education Literacy and Numeracy Strategy (NIELNS) Report of MCEETYA Taskforce on Indigenous Education	*NIELNS*'s aim was for Indigenous students to obtain literacy and numeracy levels comparable to non-Indigenous Australians. Strategies involved raising attendance rates, addressing health problems, attracting good teachers with effective teaching approaches. The *MCEETYA* report was a formal acknowledgment of deficiencies and issues in Indigenous education. *MCEETYA* research identified culturally appropriate and culturally inclusive teaching as vital for improved learning outcomes for Indigenous students.
2003	Second National Report to Parliament on Indigenous Education and Training	The first report was in 2001, with the government providing $468 million for Indigenous Education both years.
2005	Aboriginal Languages Syllabus for NSW Schools	The goals of the *NSW Aboriginal Languages Syllabus* from Kindergarten to Year10 included students gaining language skills and understanding the relationship between land, language, culture and identity.
2008	Aboriginal Education and Training Policy	This policy implemented by the *NSW Department of Education* aimed at improving educational outcomes for Indigenous students in all educational settings by enhancing cultural education for teaching staff, working together with Aboriginal communities and providing Aboriginal education for all Australian students.
2010–2014	Aboriginal and Torres Strait Islander Education Action Plan 2010–2014	The plan identified six domains at the national, systemic and local level in order to improve learning outcomes for ATSI students. These included engagement and readiness for school, attendance, leadership, literacy and numeracy, and pathways after school.
2013	Australian Curriculum	The national curriculum strove to equalize education across Australia. Its rationale included improving equity, quality and transparency in the education system. The Australian Curriculum listed Aboriginal and Torres Strait Islander Histories and Cultures as one of its cross-curriculum priorities. It aimed at reflecting Aboriginal identity and culture in the curriculum and improving Aboriginal students' learning outcomes to correspond to those of their non-Aboriginal peers. Aboriginal perspectives should be incorporated in teaching and learning to support efforts towards respect, recognition and reconciliation of Indigenous worldviews.

2015	National Aboriginal and Torres Strait Islander Education Strategy 2015	The Education Strategy aimed at improving the education and life outcomes of Australia's First Nations peoples: "All Aboriginal and Torres Strait Islander children and young people will achieve their full learning potential, are empowered to shape their own futures and are supported to embrace their culture and identity as Australia's First Nation peoples" (Education Council 2017, 4). Building on the educational principles of equity, accountability and leadership, cultural recognition and identity, relationships and partnerships, local approaches and quality teaching, the core dimensions of the Education Strategy included: • Literacy & Numeracy (Australian Curriculum) • Attendance • Transition Points (pathways) • School and Child Readiness
2020	National Agreement on Closing the Gap	Through a collaboration between the Australian governments and Indigenous Australian communities and organizations, 17 long-term goals were determined to overcome inequality and improve life outcomes of Indigenous Australian people, i.e. "close the gap." Three of them were the following: • Children are engaged in high quality, culturally appropriate early childhood education in their early years (by 2025) • People maintain a distinctive cultural, spiritual, physical and economic relationship with their land and waters (by 2030) • Cultures and languages are strong, supported and flourishing (by 2031)

Table 8: Policies Affecting Indigenous Education[22]

Looking at the status and the treatment of Indigenous Australian languages in history, different types of policies can be identified in Table 8 with reference to the policies discussed in Chapter II.3.3. For

---

[22] Data retrieved from Closing the Gap in Partnership 2020; NSW Department of Education 2020; Morisson et al 2019, 8–9; Education Council 2015, 3–4; Sarra 2011, 176–180; McKay 2007, 114–115; Zubrick et al. 2006, 41–43; Board of Studies NSW 2010; Australian Curriculum, Assessment and Reporting Authority, n.d.b.

instance, it can be presumed that Churchill's (1986) stage one policies in Australia prevailed until the 1970s. The period of the *Stolen Generation* could therefore be considered an extreme realization of level two policies, demonstrating a greatly assimilationist perspective. Overall, the National Aboriginal and Torres Strait Islander Education Policy, which was implemented in 1990, is regarded as one of the most significant developments in First Nations education today. The policy constitutes the first national policy to address disparities in educational outcomes while aiming at equity and justice at all levels of education. The 21 goals include, among other aspects, the connection of schools with Aboriginal communities, the involvement of Indigenous Australians in decision making and goal setting, and equity in access to and participation in education (Morisson et al. 2019, 8). In spite of this, it was criticized for neglecting to include potential reasons for the divergent academic success rates between Indigenous and non-Indigenous students. In relation to Churchill's (1986) typology, it may thus be categorized as an example of a stage three policy. Hence, several deficiencies in educational approaches still existed and could be attributed to a lack of understanding and/or commitment to lasting change.

These issues were addressed in a report by the Ministerial Council on Education, Employment, Training and Youth Affairs (MCEETYA) published in 2000, outlining the broader disadvantages faced by Aboriginal people that hindered successful learning. Despite several policies aimed at supporting Indigenous Australian students' learning in class, schools and teachers struggled to implement the principles and approaches (Zubrick et al. 2006, 39–41).

Evidently, changes in the Australian education system that showed links to Churchill's fourth type of policies were made after the turn of the century, during a time when Australia demonstrated a renewed interest in multilingualism and multiculturalism (Liddicoat 2009, 190–201). As such, the Aboriginal Languages Syllabus, published in 2005, aimed at the development of Indigenous language competences and a sound understanding of Indigenous cultures for all students in NSW schools. Similarly, by means of the

Aboriginal Education and Training Policy of 2008, educational outcomes of Indigenous learners were to be improved through proper culture training of teaching staff, close collaborations with communities and the inclusion of Aboriginal education in all schools.

The national Australian Curriculum, published in 2013, aimed at unifying both the rationale and objectives of education across the country. The curriculum itself was divided into learning areas, general capabilities as well as cross-curriculum priorities. At the beginning, the curriculum listed intercultural understanding as a key capability with which all Australian learners should be equipped. Figure 6 illustrates the elements of intercultural understanding as conceptualized in this policy document:

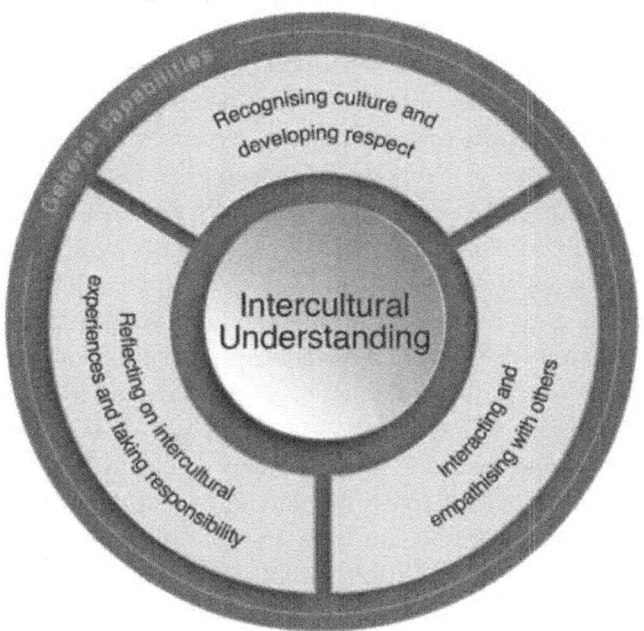

Figure 6: Intercultural Understanding in the Australian Curriculum[23]

Fundamentally, the National Curriculum outlined the following imperative in connection with intercultural understanding:

---

[23] Image retrieved from ACARA, n.d.a.

> [S]tudents develop intercultural understanding as they learn to value their own cultures, languages and beliefs, and those of others. They come to understand how personal, group and national identities are shaped, and the variable and changing nature of culture. Intercultural understanding involves students learning about and engaging with diverse cultures in ways that recognise commonalities and differences, create connections with others and cultivate mutual respect. Intercultural understanding is an essential part of living with others in the diverse world of the twenty-first century. It assists young people to become responsible local and global citizens, equipped through their education for living and working together in an interconnected world. (ACARA, n.d.a)

The reflection of Aboriginal identity and culture in the document is of particular relevance for First Nations perspectives as it listed Aboriginal and Torres Strait Islander Histories and Cultures as one of three cross-curriculum priorities in education. Specifically, the curriculum demanded that teachers incorporate culturally responsive approaches and Indigenous Australian perspectives in their practice to support efforts towards respect, recognition, and reconciliation of Indigenous worldviews (Morisson et al. 2019, 8–9; Australian Curriculum, Assessment and Reporting Authority, n.d.b). "Through the Australian Curriculum, students will understand that contemporary Aboriginal and Torres Strait Islander communities are strong, resilient, rich and diverse" (ACARA, n.d.b). Specifically, the curriculum provided a conceptual framework for learning, which incorporated the interrelated dimensions of people, country/place as well as culture. This framework was deemed vital for strengthening learners' identities and community connections since "all students gain access to knowledge and understanding of Australia that can only come from an Aboriginal or Torres Strait Islander perspective" (ACARA, n.d.b). Table 9 outlines the underlying beliefs expressed in the framework characterizing the individual dimensions:

Country/Place	• Australia has two distinct Indigenous groups: Aboriginal peoples and Torres Strait Islander peoples, and significant diversity exists within those groups. • Aboriginal and Torres Strait Islander communities maintain a special connection to and responsibility for Country/Place. • Aboriginal and Torres Strait Islander peoples have holistic belief systems and are spiritually and intellectually connected to the land, sea, sky and waterways.
Culture	• Aboriginal and Torres Strait Islander societies have many Language Groups. • Aboriginal and Torres Strait Islander peoples' ways of life are uniquely expressed through ways of being, knowing, thinking, and doing. • Aboriginal and Torres Strait Islander peoples live in Australia as first peoples of Country or Place and demonstrate resilience in responding to historic and contemporary impacts of colonization.
People	• The broader Aboriginal and Torres Strait Islander societies encompass a diversity of nations across Australia. • Aboriginal and Torres Strait Islander peoples' family and kinship structures are strong and sophisticated. • The significant contributions of Aboriginal and Torres Strait Islander peoples in the present and past are acknowledged locally, nationally and globally.

Table 9: Conceptual Framework for Learning in the Australian Curriculum[24]

One objective of the Australian curriculum with regards to Indigenous learners related to language revitalization:

> For Aboriginal and Torres Strait Islander students, learning their own language can have a significant influence on their overall learning and achievements. It can foster a strong sense of identity, pride and self-esteem and enables students to develop a wider recognition and understanding of their culture, Country/Place and People. This then contributes to their wellbeing. (ACARA, n.d.b)

Building on efforts expressed in the National Curriculum, one of the two most recent national policy documents relating to Indigenous perspectives in education is the National Aboriginal and

---

[24]   Data retrieved from ACARA, n.d.b.

Torres Strait Islander Education Strategy 2015. Upon closer inspection, the latter document does not reveal considerable differences when compared with the Aboriginal and Torres Strait Islander Education Action Plan 2010–2014, again fostering literacy and numeracy, increasing attendance, encouraging leadership and readiness, and facilitating pathways are core goals. The Education Council emphasized the overall objective of the strategy as follows: "All Aboriginal and Torres Strait Islander children and young people will achieve their full learning potential, are empowered to shape their own futures and are supported to embrace their culture and identity as Australia's First Nation peoples" (Education Council 2017, 4).

Finally, the National Agreement on Closing the Gap was published in 2020 and emerged from close collaboration and shared decision-making between Indigenous Australian experts and government authorities. Most of the proposed 17 long-term goals looked more than a decade into the future seeking to counter inequality in various sectors, including education. These included the enhanced support for cultures and languages, the importance of keeping strong relationships with the land and the necessity to engage students in high-quality and culturally appropriate.

At this stage, Morisson et al. (2019, 9) highlight that most of Australia's policy documents attribute special importance to—and, thus, show acknowledgment of—cultural connections for Indigenous Australian learners. Despite the great number of efforts made and policies published to improve educational outcomes for Indigenous students, Sarra et al. (2018, 32) criticize the prevalent deficit positioning of the Aboriginal Australian population in policy documents.

Looking at the dimensions underpinning the learning context of Indigenous Australian students in contemporary education, recent data revealed that 240,180 learners, equaling 6% of the total student population in Australia, indicated that they were of Aboriginal or Torres Strait Islander descent in 2020. The vast majority (83.4%) of Indigenous learners in Australia attended government, i.e. public, schools. Indigenous Australian learners amounted to 6.4% of all enrollments in schools in NSW in contrast to 39% in the NT (Australian Bureau of Statistics 2021).

Measuring and contrasting educational success, the National Assessment Program—Literacy and Numeracy (NAPLAN) tests constitute a national standard which is of vital importance for contemporary education in Australia. There is an enduring discrepancy between the academic achievement of Indigenous students and that of their non-Indigenous peers, one that is particularly strong in the NT and Western Australia (Partington & Galloway 2007, 237). While "[b]etter outcomes in reading, writing and numeracy have become something of a national obsession" (Harrison et al. 2019, 234), the achievement gap in educational success is evident in the data obtained through the annual NAPLAN. The following table shows a comparison of Indigenous and non-Indigenous students' reading abilities and numeracy skills using data from the school years 2015 and 2019 and revealing the percentage of students reaching the respective national minimum standard.

NAPLAN Results	Year 7 Indigenous	Year 7 non-Indigenous	Year 9 Indigenous	Year 9 non-Indigenous
Reading				
2015	86.3%	95.7%	73.8%	90.4%
2019	77.9%	95.7%	71.7%	93.1%
Numeracy				
2015	88.0%	96.6%	87.3%	96.3%
2019	76.0%	95.6%	84.1%	96.8%

Table 10: Indigenous and non-Indigenous Students' Reading and Numeracy[25]

As can be seen in Table 10, there is a non-negligible gap between Indigenous and non-Indigenous students' reading and numeracy performance in the Australian education system. Alarmingly, the data indicates that the gap is widening, with a decrease in learning outcomes by approximately 10 percentage points among Indigenous year 7 students for reading and roughly 14 percentage points for numeracy. Consequently, the authors emphasize that "[g]overnment

---

[25] Data retrieved from ACARA 2019, 2015.

measures designed to indicate educational success continue to verify that we are far from providing Indigenous students with the best compulsory education" (Baxter & Meyers 2019, 521). In a similar manner, Lowe et al. (2020, 78) highlight that contemporary educational and policy efforts "have failed to substantially shift the level of educational underachievement for a majority of these students."

Having discussed relevant policy documents in relation to Australian First Nations education, the following subchapter presents certain key dimensions that shed light on teaching and learning practices in Indigenous communities.

2. Foundations of Indigenous Teaching and Learning

It is vital to note that due to the great diversity within Indigenous Australia and the numerous influences every individual is exposed to, Indigenous Australian students, like all students, do not have a preference for a single unified learning style. In this regard, Vass (2018, 98) notes that "the practices associated with learning style theory could potentially be relevant for any student, irrespective of their background, raising concerns about the dangers of singling Indigenous students out in these ways." However, Aboriginal scholar Yunkaporta points out that it "is true that all Aboriginal languages are different and carry their own ways and values, but we also have many things in common" (Yunkaporta 2010, 38). Generally, Hughes et al. (2004, 202) observe that "Aboriginal children are able performers on tasks related to their cultural knowledge and life-style, and which are presented in ways which take account of cultural expectations of courtesies and familiarity."

Authors in the field have identified certain culture-related tendencies and learning practices that have been shown to be preferred by Indigenous rather than non-Indigenous Australian students and that teachers and schools consequently should be mindful of. In this context, Hughes et al. re-emphasize the necessity for teachers to note that "Aboriginal students, regardless of whether they are from urban, rural or traditional-oriented families, have a distinctive cultural heritage. This culture informs and shapes their worldview, their values and social practices" (Hughes et al. 2004, 281).

Building on the cultural dimensions discussed in Chapter III.3.2, Table 11 contrasts tendencies in cultural approaches to teaching and learning in Indigenous and non-Indigenous communities.

Tendencies in Indigenous Learning	Tendencies in Non-Indigenous Learning
Learning by doing	Learning to do
Group achievement	Individual performance
Cooperation	Competition
Observation, imitation, trial and error	Verbal and written instruction
Situational, real-life learning	Practice in stilted settings
Concrete	Abstract
Holistic	Sequential/analytic
Spontaneous	Structured
Contextualized	Decontextualized
Person-oriented	Information-oriented
Indirect questioning	Direct questioning

Table 11: Tendencies in Indigenous and non-Indigenous Learning Practices[26]

As illustrated above, working with visual and concrete material is frequently favored by Indigenous learners. Moreover, as seen in Chapter III.3.2, teamwork and collaboration are highly valued in First Nations cultures and story sharing is used as means to obtain and exchange information. As most non-Indigenous contexts are generally characterized by direct questions and answers and most formal school contexts require abstract thinking and written discourses, these dimensions already constitute two of numerous aspects that can make schooling particularly challenging for Indigenous Australian students (Hughes et al. 2004, 201–203).

The following sections investigate three exemplary cultural concepts that have been identified as essential for Indigenous Australian students' learning.

2.1 Relationships

First and foremost, Yunkaporta (2010, 38) describes First Nations Australian worldviews as follows:

---

[26] Data retrieved from Hughes, More, and Williams 2004, 238–240.

> From our language and our land knowledge we know there are always connections among all things, places where different elements are no longer separate but mix together and become something else. This way of working gives us new innovations as well as bringing us together.

In this regard, Donovan (2015, 629), among others, highlights the building of strong relationships as a key feature in learning contexts involving Indigenous students. Sarra et al. (2018) move beyond this demand by calling for the development of *high-expectations relationships* between Indigenous and non-Indigenous Australia in their elaborations. Labeling it a *strength-based approach*, the authors explain that the "notion of high expectations emerged to counter the pervasive deficit discourse in Indigenous education" (Sarra et al. 2018, 33) (see section 4.2). Specifically, the concept refers to relationships that are both supportive and challenging and that encourage students "to think about their own strengths and find their own tools and strategies to have greater resilience, tolerance and acceptance" (Sarra et al. 2018, 41). As a consequence, in a high-expectations approach,

> cultural differences are celebrated, and strength-based conversations provide a solid basis for group members to work together to cocreate solutions. Yarning circles enable spaces for dialogue where ideas can be challenged, and multiple perspectives enact collective sense-making and consensual decision making. When the thinking, conversing and behaviours that build high-expectations relationships become cultural practices within a school, the quality of collegiate staff environments, strong teacher-student relationships and relationships with parents and community are all enhanced. (Sarra et al. 2018, 42)

Due to the specific significance of relationships for Indigenous learning, different schools have adopted relationship building as a core principle (see section 4.). *Yarning* as well as the closely-related concept of *storytelling* are discussed in the next section.

2.2 Storytelling and Yarning

Fundamentally, "[s]torytelling is culturally relevant to every First Nations community and is an important life skill valued by the community's traditional practice of an oral history and oral language" (Peltier 2010, 11). In this context, Yunkaporta (2020, 152–153) outlines the difference between print-based and oral cultures in the following manner:

> Oral cultures are known as high-context or field-dependent-reasoning cultures. They have no isolated variables: all thinking is dependent on the field or context. Print-based cultures, by contrast, are low-context or field-independent-reasoning cultures. This is because they remain independent of the field or context, focusing on ideas and objects in isolation.

Generally, for both Aboriginal and non-Aboriginal people, knowledge is retained and handed down by means of stories (Yunkaporta 2009, 31), and knowledge and insights into Indigenous worldviews can be gained by means of narratives (Peltier 2010). According to Malcolm (2018, 10), storytelling is an "essential element of Aboriginal cultural life."

Moreover, "[s]tories are told for pleasure and relaxation but may also serve instructive or moral purposes" (Malcolm 2018, 10). The art of storytelling thus constitutes a significant educational approach and is also featured as a central dimension in Yunkaporta's identified eight ways of Aboriginal learning (see Chapter IV.3.1). By including personal narratives and orality in learning processes and thus replicating the way Elders have passed on knowledge, which Yunkaporta (2011, 49) refers to as *story sharing*, respect is paid to Aboriginal cultures and Indigenous students receive greater opportunities to participate in class (Peltier 2010, 12–18). Finally, the closely-related concept of *yarning* relates to "talking seriously about a matter of concern" (Malcolm 2018, 116).

In addition to relationships and storytelling, a third cultural dimension to be discussed in this chapter is the concept of *shame*. As the concept can cause great damage to First Nations students' self-esteem and, consequently, can constitute a barrier to learning, it is essential for teachers to gain awareness of what it comprises. Thus, the concept is examined in the following section.

2.3 The Concept of Shame

In a non-Indigenous context, shame or feeling ashamed usually relate to some form of misconduct or inappropriate behavior. In contrast, the "Aboriginal English word shame can refer to a variety of situations, particularly when a person is singled out from a group, whether for rebuke or for praise" (Eades 2014, 429). Like Eades, Malcolm and Truscott (2012, 229) also highlight that "[i]t is shame, to an Aboriginal student, to be discriminated from the group, to be individually focused on, whether by being shown to be lacking in knowledge or skill, or by being credited with higher achievement than the group." In her elaborations, Harkins (1994, 158) identifies several factors that can provoke shame in Indigenous Australian learners:

- the feeling of not belonging in a specific place or near a specific person
- the anxiety of people's sentiments, of doing the wrong thing, or of the consequences of an action
- the strong wish to escape this inconvenient situation

Hence, the concept of shame constitutes one of various dimensions that teachers need to be mindful of to foster Indigenous students' learning in school. To conclude, Hughes et al. (2004, 249) state that "[e]ducation for Aboriginal students will only be fully successful when it values their culture and traditions, and when teaching is adapted to their characteristics and learning styles." Therefore, different frameworks have been proposed to assist teachers in making their classroom practice more culturally sensitive to Indigenous learners. A selection of three pedagogies is presented in the following section.

3. Proposed Frameworks and Pedagogies

Since "Australian classrooms are increasingly culturally and linguistically diverse, yet the evidence suggests that many teachers lack the confidence and/or expertise to engage with cultural difference in supportive and educationally productive ways" (Morisson et al. 2019, 57), different authors have proposed frameworks and models to assist teachers.

3.1 Eight Ways of Aboriginal Learning

In his work, Yunkaporta stresses that non-Indigenous educators face a challenging task when working with Indigenous Australian children. While some of the teachers might know what Aboriginal students value and why it is essential to consider and incorporate certain dimensions in class, little guidance on how to do so in practice exists (2009, 5). In his role as an Aboriginal scholar, Yunkaporta therefore endeavored to create a comprehensible framework for Aboriginal pedagogy to support classroom teachers in learning about Aboriginal knowledge and integrating it into the classroom, which has established a vital starting point for inclusive education.

In his model, "Indigenous knowledges are presented as a sophisticated system and an effective way to embed Indigenous knowledges into curriculum and pedagogy" (Burgess et al. 2019, 308). Building on his observations exploring Aboriginal ways of knowing, being, and doing in western NSW, Yunkaporta (2010) therefore proposes eight ways of Aboriginal learning to be implemented in educational settings, albeit emphasizing their particular relevance for Aboriginal language classrooms. Specifically, he accentuates the importance of learning through rather than about culture and thereby of putting the focus on the process rather than the content of learning. Furthermore, he claims that the eight perspectives demonstrate common ground and shared pedagogical features among many cultural groups that educators of any community can make use of to promote intercultural learning (Yunkaporta 2009, 45–46). His model is visualized in the following figure:

Figure 7: Eight Ways of Aboriginal Learning[27]

---

[27] Image retrieved from Yunkaporta 2010, 40.

Figure 7 demonstrates the interconnectedness of the eight concepts of learning, which compose one dynamic entity. These eight concepts are briefly explained below.

The first way of learning, *Story Sharing*, is concerned with "teaching and learning through narrative" (Yunkaporta 2009, 35). In the classroom, students can tell their personal stories and thereby draw on their home culture and knowledge, which creates the content for the (language) lesson. The teacher can start by sharing their own story as a model and learners can be given more or less guidance in the class. Further in-class activities should then be related to the shared stories.

Learning Maps look at the visualization of steps in learning processes and make certain structures and activities tangible for students. A third perspective in the pedagogy is *Non-verbal* learning denoting a more hands-on approach and the use of body language and silence in class. This way of learning promotes students' self-reliance and fosters their critical thinking. *Symbols and Images* should be used to facilitate the students' understanding of contents and to explore materials more vividly. As Aboriginal students are predominantly visual learners, symbols and both concrete and abstract imagery can greatly support their learning processes.

The fifth dimension of Yunkaporta's Aboriginal pedagogy is *Land Links*, referring to the connection between teaching contents and the area and place fostering the strong bond Aboriginal Australians have with the land. In addition to non-verbal learning, the *Non-linear* concept supports the idea of non-sequential learning processes, since indirect approaches and learning cycles are important Aboriginal ways of working with knowledge domains.

A seventh way of incorporating Aboriginal learning strategies is concerned with processes of deconstructing and reconstructing. Teachers should find a balance between instruction and independent work and support deductive learning, i.e. learning whole concepts before breaking them down into their parts. *Deconstruct/Reconstruct* thus emphasizes the importance of holistic, scaffolded and self-contained learning.

Finally, by means of *Community Links*, teachers endeavor to incorporate the local communities' values and knowledge into learning and apply a group-oriented pedagogy connected with real-life contexts (Yunkaporta 2009, 34–38, 47–50).

Since his approach is positioned at the "interface of two worlds" (Yunkaporta 2010, 38), Yunkaporta also proposes the following boomerang matrix to illustrate how greater knowledge of the dynamics and characteristics of Aboriginal and non-Aboriginal cultures provides a common ground for mutual understanding and respect (Figure 8):

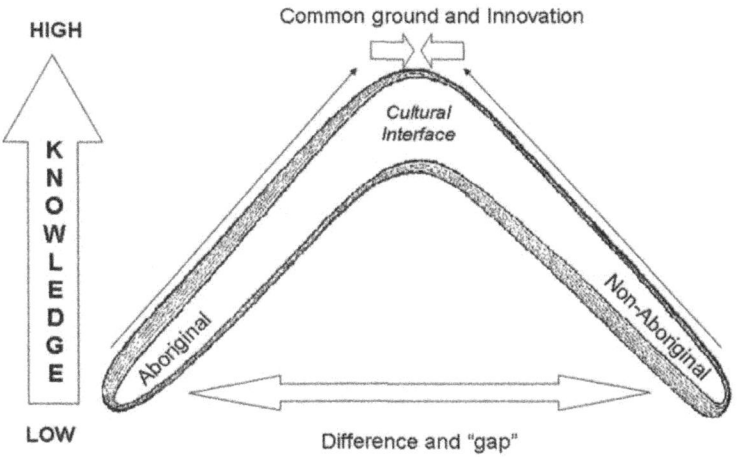

Figure 8: The Boomerang Matrix[28]

Yunkaporta (2009, 50) ultimately states that "explicit Aboriginal pedagogy is needed to improve outcomes for Indigenous learners." He also believes that "there is common ground between Aboriginal pedagogies and the optimal pedagogies for all learners" (Yunkaporta 2009, 50). In conclusion, he highlights the imperative to abandon tokenistic inclusion of cultural dimensions so that cultural knowledge is not (only) about *what* is taught but is increasingly invested in *how* it is taught. Yunkaporta thus concludes: "We need to learn *through* culture, not just *about* culture" (Yunkaporta 2010, 48).

---

[28] Image retrieved from Yunkaporta 2009, 4.

3.2 Culturally Nourishing Pedagogy

In a recent publication, Lowe et al. (2020) propose culturally nourishing pedagogy as a fruitful approach to do justice to Indigenous Australian learners' cultural backgrounds. The individual dimensions of this approach are visualized in Figure 9.

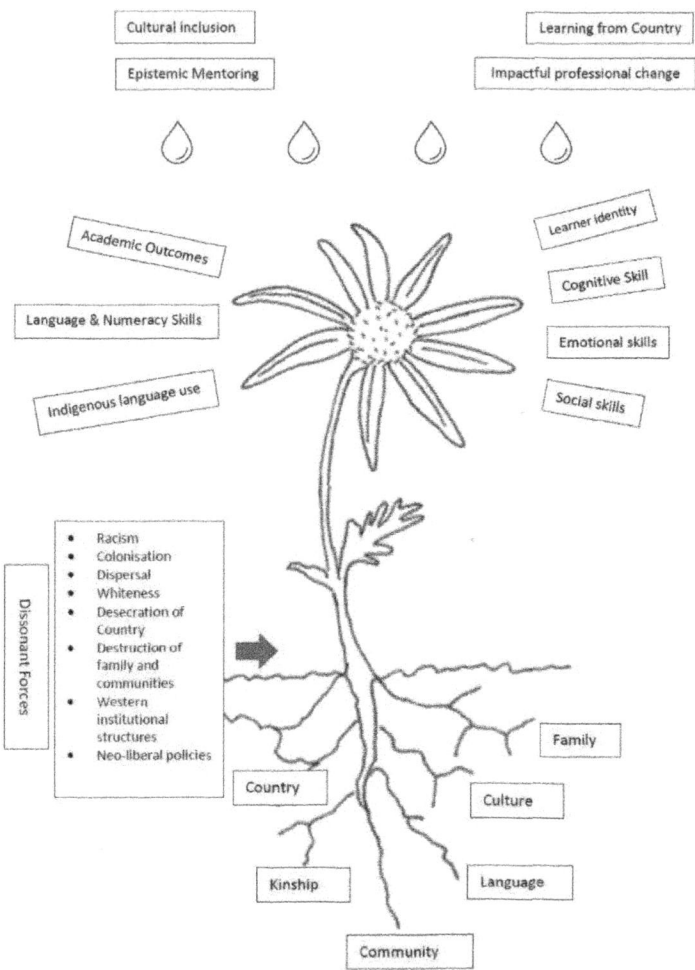

Figure 9: The Framework of Culturally Nourishing Pedagogy[29]

---

[29] Image retrieved from Lowe et al. 2020, 3.

The authors thus identify four key elements, illustrated as raindrops in Figure 9, which are essential for providing a culturally nourishing pedagogy in classrooms across Australia. These are outlined below (Table 12):

Learning from Country	Cultural Inclusion	Epistemic Monitoring	Impactful Professional Change
• Country as a teacher of Indigenous stories, cultures and worldviews • Creating a sense of belonging • Learning through relationships • Learning as an ongoing process • Place-based learning	• Acknowledging the importance of including Indigenous cultural and linguistic heritage and of implementing Indigenous practices • Community/family involvement and relationship building • Strengthening learners' identity • Non-tokenistic but intertwined with other elements of schooling	• Indigenous people mentoring non-Aboriginal educators • Implementing culturally responsive approaches • Countering assimilationist tendencies in education • Community-led workshops increasing awareness and willingness	• Enabling critical understanding of past and present policy failures • Improving quality of teaching using the three dimensions to propel systemic and structural change in education • Overcoming the deficit paradigm and racialized pedagogies

Table 12: The Four Pillars of Culturally Nourishing Pedagogy[30]

Generally, Lowe et al. (2020) emphasize the call to adopt holistic, whole-school approaches that rethink leadership dimensions, connect with Aboriginal families, foster educators' professional learning, enact culturally nourishing approaches and establish the necessary pillars to undertake these strategies. Lowe et al. (2020, 2) thus conclude:

---

[30] Data retrieved from Lowe et al. 2020, 3–11.

We believe that whole of school initiatives that genuinely engage in depth with these four elements, as intertwined and interrelated parts of a living localized learning community, will more likely result in educational experiences that improve the academic achievements of Indigenous students, while also further strengthening their identities and connections to place.

3.3 Culturally Responsive Pedagogy

Based on their comprehensive literature review, Morisson et al. (2019, 58) plead for the realization and adoption of culturally responsive pedagogies, which "embrace and build on students' identities and backgrounds as assets for learning." Combining research studies conducted at primary and secondary metropolitan government schools in Australia, where most Indigenous Australian students receive their formal education (Australian Bureau of Statistics 2021), Morrison et al. (2019, 11) summarize that Aboriginal students desire:

- strong, trustworthy and mutually respectful relationships with their teachers
- culturally safe spaces
- recognition and valuing of Aboriginal identity and culture
- an ethos of high expectations, instead of deficit views

Inside increasingly diverse Australian classrooms, the authors identify conceptual confusions, super-diversity, essentialism and stereotyping, tokenistic/superficial approaches, self-determination and fear (Morisson et al. 2019, 43–51) as hindrances for the successful adoption of culturally responsive education. However, the approach is necessary for "improving learning experiences and outcomes for Aboriginal young people, for students from diverse heritages, and indeed for *all* students in Australian schools" (Morisson et al. 2019, 58).

4. Adopted Approaches in Australian Schools

Building on the frameworks outlined in Chapter II.3 and Chapter IV.3, this section presents approaches which attend to First Nations perspectives and which are implemented in specific Australian schools. These are examples and do not constitute an exhaustive list of existing approaches in Australia.

4.1 Two-way Schooling

One approach implemented in the Australian school system that considers linguistic and cultural dimensions in connection with Indigenous Australian learners is the two-way education model (see Chapter II.3.2.1). Fundamentally, Harris (1990, 14) states that a two-way school "should provide for the skills and knowledge from both cultures to be learned; all involving a source of knowledge, a style of doing things, and learning contexts which authentically match each body of learning." In Australia, two-way Aboriginal schools aim at supporting Indigenous Australian students in becoming bicultural. The schools typically differentiate between Indigenous and non-Indigenous domains and a lot of autonomy is assigned to the instructors in order to authentically represent their respective cultures while the local Aboriginal community retains the highest authority over school-related matters. In an Aboriginal two-way school, Indigenous teachers need to strongly represent and embody traditional language and culture while non-Indigenous instructors should impart Western values and teach Standard English. This approach ensures that Aboriginal students learn to adjust to the cultural needs of certain situations in life in addition to retaining a strong Aboriginal identity (ibid., 13–18). Generally, Harris (1990, 48) regards the two-way Aboriginal school as an

> opportunity for the primary Aboriginal identity to stay strong, though changing and thus continue to be the source of inner strength and security necessary for dealing with the Western world. Two-way schooling should help to keep the option of living in an Aboriginal world more truly open.

Consequently, two-way programs arguably could be regarded sub-branches of bilingual education. However, Harris (1990) states that a clear difference between the two exists, since bilingual education can be implemented by non-Aboriginal people, whereas two-way Aboriginal teaching can only be initiated by Aboriginal educators. Hence, he concludes that two-way schools can promote long-term biculturalism if they are structured to reflect and promote living and learning in two culture domains (ibid., 19).

In the 1980s, Eagleson, Kaldor and Malcolm proposed the approach of Teaching Standard English as a Second Dialect with the aim of supporting learners with AE as their first language to become proficient in SAE, "while making sure that successful and meaningful communication takes place between teacher and child from the first day at school" (Eagleson et al. 1982, 196, cited in Eades 2014, 426). Their approach consists of the following three dimensions: Learning about Indigenous Australian culture and traditions, listening carefully to the content of children's speech, and appreciating AE and creoles as assets rather than obstacles in the learning of SAE. In spite of their efforts, however, the approach was generally not adopted by teachers (Eades 2014, 426).

4.1.1 Two-way Bidialectal Education

More recently, a variation merging the two-way approach with bidialectal education, the so-called *two-way bidialectal education*, was introduced and investigated by Malcolm and Truscott (2012). The authors describe their approach as follows:

> The approach is two-way in that both Aboriginal and non-Aboriginal staff work on it together, and in that it envisages that both Aboriginal and non-Aboriginal students will be engaged in learning from one another and from their respective dialects. It is bidialectal, in that it recognizes Aboriginal students' need for communicative competence and literacy in both Aboriginal English and SAE. (Malcolm & Truscott 2012, 232)

In contrast to the original two-way rationale, Malcolm and Truscott (2012) also include the perspectives and learning experiences of non-Aboriginal students in their evidence-based approach, something rarely undertaken in First Nations education. The two-way bidialectal model therefore "also recognizes non-Aboriginal students' need for at least passive communicative competence in Aboriginal English (for the sake of mutual comprehension, cross-cultural understanding and respect) in addition to literacy in SAE" (ibid., 232). The table below shows the underlying theory and objectives of the two-way bidialectal approach and outlines how teachers, principals, and students can work and learn together successfully.

	Aim	School/Principal	Teacher	Aboriginal Staff	Students
Relationship Building	To motivate communication	(a) Community Contact • reciprocal visitation • cross-generation relationship (b) School Policy • cross-cultural sensitivity • use of Aboriginal English (c) Staff development • enculturation of staff (d) Bicultural school environment	(a) Empowerment of Aboriginal staff • shared planning • class role (b) Openness to appropriate use of Aboriginal English (home language – HL) (c) Class Policy • mutual respect building • mutual cultural learning • mutual dialect acceptance (d) Classroom environment	(a) Community Contact • with principal independently (b) Providing input to teacher • on student communication • on cultural sensitivities • on learning materials (c) Providing input and counselling to students	(a) Reciprocal respectful relationship building (b) Reciprocal cultural learning (c) Working in bicultural pairs and groups (d) Equal access to empowerment through election of school councilors
Mutual Comprehension Building	To facilitate communication	(a) Staffing • appointing sufficient Aboriginal staff • providing appropriate bicultural staff induction (b) Staff development • performance management (c) Resourcing • allocating time • funding resources	(a) Classroom Organization (b) Organizing learning in small groups and pairs (c) Exploiting bidialectal competence of Aboriginal staff (d) Mutual sociolinguistic enabling (e) Developing cross-dialectal listening skills	(a) Providing interpretation and translation to teacher (b) Providing interpretation to students as needed (c) Assisting in modifying learning materials (d) Assisting in classroom enculturation of students (e) Counselling disaffected students	(a) Assisting culturally different students with mutual expression and understanding (b) Learning from culturally diverse materials (c) Acquiring cross-dialectal listening and comprehension skills

Repertoire Building	To expand communication	(a) Mandating recognition of prior English learning in literacy instruction (b) Incorporating bidialectal competencies in school assessment policy (c) Promotion of bias-free ways of referring to HL	(a) Designated HL time (b) Bidialectal learning resources (developed or modified) (c) Bidialectal learning strategies (d) Multi-modal communicative support (e) Celebrating bidialectalism	(a) Modeling Aboriginal English (b) Modeling code-switching (c) Alerting teachers to cross-dialectal conceptual mismatches	(a) Aboriginal students developing active bidialectal skills including biliteracy and code-switching (b) Non-Aboriginal students developing passive bidialectal skills
Skill Building	To enhance learning	(a) Providing literacy materials for home use (b) Providing time for modification of SAE learning materials (c) Ongoing professional development for all (d) Rewarding biliteracy	(a) Bridging from established HL literacy to SAE literacy (b) Exploit teaching of dimensions of dialect contrast (c) Biliteracy learning resources (d) Systematic recording of SAE progress (d) Bidialectal assessment	(a) Assessing with bidialectal assessment (b) Ongoing feedback to teachers on student learning problems (c) Ongoing feedback to community on student progress	(a) Peer feedback in pairs or groups (b) Using appropriate home literacy materials (c) Setting progressive achievement goals

Table 13: Two-way Bidialectal Education with Practical Outworking[31]

---

[31] Modified from Malcolm & Truscott 2012, 235.

Reviewing Table 13, Malcolm and Truscott (2012) describe the process of *relationship building* between Aboriginal and non-Aboriginal students as a vital first step towards creating a school that fosters both cultural groups and their respective dialects. The principal is assigned a major role in this process and should ensure that non-Aboriginal teachers are sensitized to cultural conventions and learning behaviors of Aboriginal students.

Mutual comprehension building constitutes a further step in this two-way bidialectal approach to teaching and learning. This dimension includes the importance of having bicultural staff members, especially Aboriginal teachers, to help facilitate communication in classrooms by assisting other teachers with their learning materials and modes of instruction. The third aspect, *repertoire building*, addresses the importance of promoting Aboriginal speakers' dialectal richness while ensuring their acquisition of literacy in the first dialect before extending the latter.

A last dimension Malcolm and Truscott (2012) identify in two-way bidialectal learning concerns *skill building* in Standard Australian English. The authors consider proficiency in SAE as vital for future learning, though they clearly promote modifications of teaching materials to make them appropriate for all learners (233–237).

Investigating the implementation of the two-way approach across schools in WA, Malcolm (2018, 197–199) identifies four major aims of two-way education: motivating communication, facilitating communication, expanding communication, and enhancing learning. Moreover, he observes the following key characteristics of the applied classroom practices in the schools investigated (ibid.):

- Proceeding from the known to the unknown
- Elimination of cultural bias in teaching and testing
- Additive rather than subtractive language instruction
- Interdependence of language competencies
- Identity support rather than opposition
- Exploitation of linguistic/cultural diversity as a classroom/life/learning resource
- Community engagement and relationship-building
- Two-Way Principle

4.1.2 Worawa Aboriginal College

Founded in 1983, this girls-only boarding school near Melbourne was the first Aboriginal school in Victoria and has been managed and owned by Aboriginal people. Apart from looking at students' physical health and well-being particularly, the two-way model adopted at Worawa Aboriginal College consists of four interrelated cultural concepts: relationship, responsibility, respect, and rigor. These values strongly represent Aboriginal ways of knowing, being, and doing, and are essential for ensuring the students' well-being and strong self-esteem as well as a productive learning environment with the goal of *walking together to make a difference*.

A case study conducted by Hamilton (2015) at Worawa Aboriginal College focuses on factors that students and adults at the school identified as either nurturing or challenging for learning. Among other aspects, the study shows that empowerment was achieved through nurturing culture and building respectful relationships between students, staff, and families in order to generate confidence and a sense of belonging. Moreover, holding high but achievable expectations of the students, giving them opportunities to participate meaningfully in class, and fostering their belief in themselves were identified as further vital factors for student learning. Hamilton's investigations also highlight that the approaches at Worawa Aboriginal College were greatly influenced by Yunkaporta's pedagogy (see section 3.1). The key enabling factors for efficient learning in school are identified as a strong teacher commitment, Aboriginal leadership, and personalized learning to foster a balanced two-way pedagogy that values both the Aboriginal and non-Aboriginal Australian culture alike. Hamilton (2015) argues that all students throughout Australia would benefit greatly from such a two-way approach to teaching and learning by incorporating the values of relationship, responsibility, respect, and rigor.

4.2 The Stronger Smarter Approach

Looking at further strategies that are concerned with First Nations students' learning, the *Strong and Smart* pedagogy and the *Stronger Smarter Institute* were introduced by Aboriginal educationalist

Chris Sarra and aim at strengthening Aboriginal identities, self-esteem, and pride through schooling.

Before its implementation in several schools across Australia, the approach was initially applied at Cherbourg State School, an Aboriginal School in Queensland where Sarra was appointed as the first Aboriginal principal in 1998. The *Stronger Smarter Approach* acknowledges the need for schools to challenge, develop, and embrace Aboriginal identity in order for Aboriginal students to become strong and smart. Table 14 illustrates what these three concepts comprise:

Concept	Description
Challenging	Students confront their Aboriginality and reflect on its disclosure in their behavior and attitudes in school Challenging teachers' perceptions of Aboriginal identity
Developing	Providing opportunities to create a more positive perception of Aboriginal identity both at the student and staff level
Embracing	School and society as places that embrace positive Aboriginal identity

Table 14: Concepts of the *Stronger Smarter Approach*[32]

By holding high expectations of the students, building strong teacher-student relationships, strongly supporting literacy skills, including Aboriginal staff, and promoting community and parent involvement, positive learner engagement effects have been achieved in schools following the Stronger Smarter Approach (Sarra et al. 2018, 33).

By means of the four key elements of the approach, including responsibility for change, strong and smart, high-expectations relationships and strength-based approaches, several dimensions of culturally responsive teaching are implemented (see Chapter IV.3.3). Similar to Lowe et al. (2020), the Stronger Smarter Approach also advocates for whole-school initiatives in which the following three spheres are combined:

---

[32] Data retrieved from Sarra 2011, 106–107.

- Personal sphere: positive identities, Indigenous leadership and regarding themselves as agents of change
- School sphere: strength-based approaches, high-expectations relationships and student engagement
- Community sphere: partnerships and collaboration

Figure 10 outlines the interconnected strategies constituting the Stronger Smarter Approach.

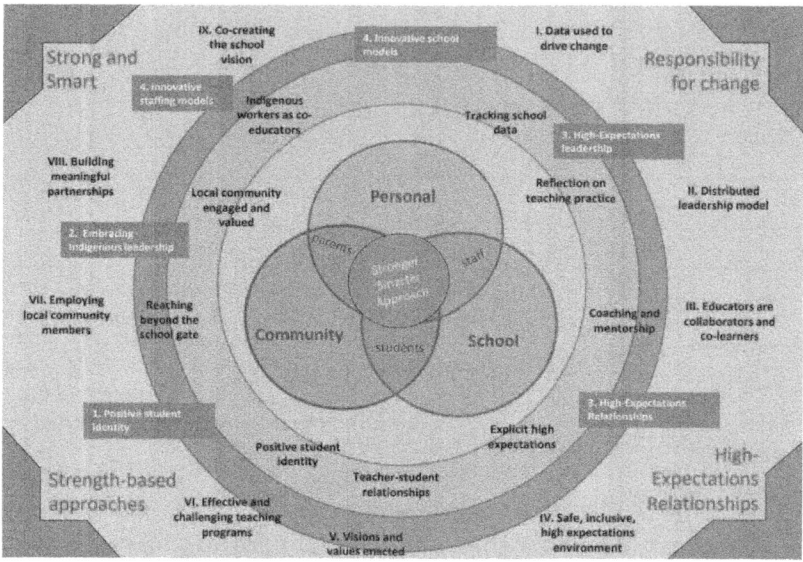

Figure 10: Strategies of the *Stronger Smarter Approach*[33]

5. Challenges in Indigenous Australian Education

Scholars in the field have identified a variety of factors that constitute impediments to Indigenous Australian students' successful learning in contemporary education. These relate to language-related obstacles, identity and culture, racism, curriculum and policy as well as teacher training, and are discussed below.

Language-related obstacles constitute a first challenge, which has been frequently discussed in literature. To start with, Malcolm

---

[33] Image retrieved from Stronger Smarter Institute 2017, 18.

(2018) describes the average Australian classroom as predominantly comprising non-Indigenous educators considering Standard Australian English as the norm. Building on this, James (2014) points out that the "standard forms of English used in school texts, speech and assessment, privileges students who have been socialised in oral Standard English in the home, and marginalises Indigenous students from vernacular backgrounds" (James 2014, 80). In addition, Malcolm and Sharifian criticize the fact that "Western-based schooling by its nature generally expects students to operate exclusively according to the schemas that underlie the 'standard' dialect" (2005, 512). As a consequence, Indigenous learners commonly respond to this reality with silence and withdrawal (Malcolm 2018, 191). In this regard, Malcolm (2018, 194) critically remarks that the predominance of monodialectal SAE classrooms does not do justice to the linguistic and communicative repertoire most Indigenous Australian learners draw on. Harkins (1994, 32) thus justly concludes that "Australia has been slow to recognize Aboriginal varieties of English as part of the wealth of our national linguistic heritage."

Shifting the focus to culture-related impediments to learning, Sarra (2011, 103) observes that "differing cultural values and beliefs brought to school by Aboriginal children and the predominantly non-Aboriginal school personnel" constitute a major challenge for Aboriginal learners. On the one hand, Indigenous learners often have a "negative sense of their own cultural identity […] with parents and community who have a negative sense of the value of schooling based on past experiences" (Sarra et al. 2018, 34). Specifically, Indigenous Australian families largely regard formal schooling and educational success to be detrimental to their children's Indigenous identities (Lowe et al. 2021, 79). On the other hand, First Nations students frequently do not consider educational achievements compatible with their cultural identities (Sarra et al. 2018, 32). Moreover, Donovan (2015, 614) observes a prevalent lack of Indigenous Australian perspectives in classroom discourse, which frequently results in learners' disengagement with school as they do not feel their identities are accepted (Donovan 2015, 614). In this regard, Hughes et al. (2004, 200) criticize the fact that

> [e]ducation systems have failed to encourage and reinforce in Australian students positive feelings and pride in their heritage and cultural identity. [...] Education has failed to recognise that [...] Aboriginal cultural values and languages are very different from those of non-Aboriginals. Current theories and methodologies are therefore largely inappropriate and this also contributes to a lack of success of Aboriginal students. The end result is institutionalised racism and assimilation, albeit unintentional and unconscious.

In this sense, Moodie et al. (2019) outline that Indigenous learners' high expectations of education at the beginning of their school careers "become difficult to sustain in the face of persistent and repeated negative representations of Indigeneity, Indigenous intelligence and academic achievement from teachers, schools and the media" (Moodie et al. 2019, 274). More specifically, the scholars enumerate withdrawal, de-identification as Indigenous Australian, emotional distress as well as the internalization of negative attitudes as some of the potential effects of racism on Indigenous learners, emphasizing that these are "harmful, wide reaching and life long, and influence academic achievement, attitudes to language, emotional wellbeing, physical health, self-concept, school attendance and post-school pathways, and eventually school choice and engagement when those students become parents" (Moodie et al. 2019, 292).

Partington (2003, 41–42) also identifies experiences with discrimination and racism in school as well as difficult life circumstances as major causes of frustration resulting in lower academic achievement rates among Indigenous learners. Specifically, Partington and Galloway (2007, 246) argue that "[f]or many Aboriginal people, at least partially as a consequence of history and policy, their background is poverty, extensive alcoholism, family dysfunction, poor health and nutrition, low aspirations and powerlessness." In a recent study, Thorpe et al. (2021, 57) express a "deep concern about the continuing disadvantage Aboriginal people experience through ongoing assimilationist education practices."

Curriculum and education policies pose a further challenge for First Nations education. Morisson et al. (2019, 7) critically remark that, until today, "education policies are overtly or covertly underpinned by deficit views of Aboriginal learners and their cultures, families and communities." Despite the inclusion of intercultural dimensions in the Australian Curriculum as well as the country's increasing cultural diversity, McCandless et al. (2020) emphasize that the education system in Australia is becoming increasingly divided due to social forces (McCandless et al. 2020, 572). Sarra (2011, 161) supports this claim by criticizing the perceived "tendency to readily accept Indigenous underachievement in schools as somehow 'normal' or 'given'" in contemporary Australian education. Hence, Morisson et al. (2019, 9) conclude that "governments are still failing to uphold their obligations to provide Aboriginal students with a culturally and linguistically appropriate education" as policies have "persistently favoured the Anglo-Australian population while marginalising the Australian Aboriginal population" (Morisson et al. 2019, 11).

In connection with diverging educational outcomes, Moodie et al. (2019, 274) observe that "[t]eachers tend to attribute problems at school to home life and diminish the impact of their own assumptions about Indigenous ability." On the contrary, Sarra (2011, 161) argues that teachers must "reflect inwards and evaluate the effectiveness of their own teaching practice and ask what it is that they are doing or not […] that contributes to Indigenous student failure" (Sarra 2011, 161). In this regard, Vass et al. (2019, 358) point to a lack of evidence-based research in connection with teachers' knowledge of and attitudes towards Indigenous culture as well as the effects and scope of deficit positioning on learners' engagement in contemporary Australian classroom discourse.

In light of these shortcomings, scholars have expressed the urgent need for revised and improved teacher education as an essential means to overcome educational disparities between Indigenous and non-Indigenous learners. Among others, Lowe et al. (2020, 10) argue that "Aboriginal students need to be empowered to resist oppressions and domination by strengthening their connections with their 'roots' that include Country, community, kinship networks, families and traditions." Therefore, Vass et al. (2019) highlight that "curricular and pedagogical practices can change in ways that value and respect the cultural wealth that students arrive at school with, and hence work more effectively with and for the Indigenous learners in the classroom" (Vass et al. 2019, 358). Moreover, "teachers need to appreciate that many Aboriginal students arrive at school with unique and valuable cultural capital, and it is the teachers who need to obtain the necessary understanding and skills to engage with these students, their parents and the local community" (Lowe et al. 2020, 10).

In their systematic literature review, Burgess et al. (2019, 312) found that impediments to the implementation of effective pedagogies are frequently connected with shortcomings in "teacher knowledge, skills and confidence in implementing." Moreover, educators predominantly need "significant support to effect the pedagogical changes needed to challenge the status quo of Indigenous underachievement, to influence school policy and establish opportunities for the inclusion of local Indigenous" (Lowe et al. 2019, 266–267). In this context, the beneficial balancing of Indigenous worldviews and the demands of the education system (Hughes et al. 2004, 230) as well as the balancing of community-specific needs and more broadly required strategies (Guenther, Harrison & Burgess 2019, 209) pose challenges for educators. Morisson et al. (2019, 47–49) emphasize the need for teachers to avoid stereotypes and refrain from adopting tokenistic approaches in relation to Indigenous Australian cultures (Morisson et al. 2019, 47–49).

In this regard, teachers should be encouraged to make use of the resources and knowledge provided by Aboriginal and Islander Education Officers who support Indigenous culture, literacy, and language development and can be significant reference persons for Indigenous students (Partington & Galloway 2007, 257–259). Generally, the authors advocate for teachers to

> challenge their knowledge of Aboriginal cultures, values and seek ways to engage with the local Aboriginal community. It will require teachers to acquire relational and pedagogic skills and to realize the centrality of learning from Country and deep cultural inclusion in their schooling practices. This positive change must come from within the system itself. (Lowe et al. 2020, 12)

Fundamentally, James (2014, 84) emphasizes that "[a]t a time of increasingly strident efforts in Australia to "close the gap" in Indigenous education, it is vital to consider how this "gap" was created and perpetuated in the first place and to pursue critical efforts to develop pedagogy that is inclusive of all learners." Evidently, "racism and colonization have produced profound inequality and contributed to unimaginable distress for Aboriginal and Torres Strait Islander peoples" (Power et al. 2015, 6). Morisson et al. (2019, 6) conclude that the

> Australian education system has served Aboriginal peoples poorly. It was — and continues to be — based on a Eurocentric model of schooling that aligns all pedagogy and curriculum to the cultural norms and values of the colonisers, imposing top down "solutions" on Aboriginal peoples with little or no consideration of Aboriginal voices, or the needs, values, interests and aspirations of Aboriginal peoples.

The authors agree that a "shift in thinking [is] needed to understand how history has impacted Indigenous education in Australia, and to move beyond essentialised cultural assumptions (such as deficit) to a more realistic and deeper understanding of the context of the individual students and their families. This opens up the possibilities for educators to change their beliefs around what is possible for high expectations in Indigenous education and their personal role in contributing to this" (Sarra et al. 2018, 42). In summary, the previously discussed issues need to be addressed in order to bring about lasting changes for Aboriginal people in the Australian education system (Partington & Galloway 2007, 259–260).

Chapter V

Research Study

This chapter comprises a comprehensive account of the explorative research study conducted, including an outline of its design and objectives as well as an in-depth presentation and discussion of the corresponding findings. Before presenting the study, a concise overview of recent research directions in the field of First Nations education in Australia is provided.

1. Current Research Directions

So far, authors in the field of Australian First Nations education have provided essential linguistic evidence for the recognition of Aboriginal English as a full dialect of SAE (Malcolm 2018; Eades 2014, 2013; Harkins 1994), investigated approaches adopted at select Australian schools by means of case studies (Stronger Smarter Institute 2017; Hamilton 2015; Malcolm & Truscott 2012), and proposed pedagogies and classroom methodologies inclusive of Indigenous Australian perspectives (Lowe et al. 2020; Morisson et al. 2019; Sarra et al. 2018; Power et al. 2015; Yunkaporta 2010). In addition, four major research areas can be identified among recent publications in the field, which cover interrelated concerns. These are outlined in Table 15 and will be discussed below.

Theme	Author(s)	Type
Exploring Indigenous Australian learners' lower literacy and academic achievement rates	Lin, Williamson, Beetson, Bartlett, Boughton & Taylor 2021	Empirical
	Guenther & Osborne 2020	Empirical
	Baxter & Meyers 2019	Empirical
Perspectives on effective teaching practices for Indigenous Australian learners	Philips & Luke 2017	Empirical
	Lewthwaite, Boon, Webber & Laffin 2017	Empirical
	Donovan 2015	Empirical
	Milgate & Giles-Browne 2013	Empirical
	Burgess, Tennent, Vass, Guenther, Lowe & Moodie 2019	Literature Review
	Lloyd, Lewthwaite, Osborne & Boon 2015	Literature Review
Improvement of pre-service teacher education	Thorpe, Burgess & Egan 2021	Empirical
	Daniels-Mayes 2020	Empirical
	Harrison, Tennent, Vass, Guenther, Lowe & Moodie 2019	Literature Review
Effects of Indigenous Language and Cultural programs	Lowe, Tennent, Moodie, Guenther & Burgess 2021	Literature Review

Table 15: Current Research Directions in First Nations Education

The first recurring theme among recent studies in Australian First Nations education is the investigation of causes for low(er) literacy and academic achievement levels among Indigenous learners. To start with, Baxter and Meyers (2019) explore the relationship between attendance and school achievement contrasting data and NAPLAN results from 76 Indigenous learners in grades 3 and 5 out of a total student population of 346 at an urban school. The evidence from the study revealed no causal relationship between school attendance and educational achievement for Indigenous Australian learners; hence, the "universal attendance and achievement relationship does not hold true" (Baxter & Meyers 2019, 527). Consequently, the authors criticize the evident discrepancy between empirical research findings and the education policies adopted and suggest further research to investigate the significance of curriculum, classroom practice, motivation and mobility for Indigenous Australian learners' educational success (Baxter & Meyers 2019, 528).

Shifting the focus to remote learning contexts, Guenther and Osborne (2020) analyze the impact of direct instruction methodology on Indigenous Australian learners' reading abilities by again drawing on their respective NAPLAN results. While the study was not able to provide evidence for an improvement of learners' literacy skills, the method's detrimental effects on Indigenous students' attendance rates were revealed. Therefore, like Baxter and Meyers (2019), the authors question the ethics of policy implementation and criticize the lack of evidence-based political decision-making.

Building on Guenther and Osborne (2020) by exploring literacy levels in eight remote Aboriginal communities in NSW, Lin et al. (2021) evaluate the long-term effects of schooling. Counterintuitively, their study reveals that the number of years of schooling completed did not correlate with enhanced reading and writing abilities. Overall, the 161 participants largely overestimated their own competences as they revealed low or very low literacy levels.

A further current research dimension is constituted by studies which incorporate views on effective schooling for Indigenous Australian learners. In the comprehensive *Dare to Lead* Project (Milgate & Giles-Browne 2013), interviews on quality practices in First Nations education were conducted with students, parents, staff, and principals at 675 schools throughout Australia. The findings of the project revealed the following core themes relevant for quality teaching practice with Indigenous Australian learners (Table 16):

Cultural Environment	Celebration of cultural identity and respect
Quality Teachers	High expectations of learners; strong relationships with learners and families
Community Engagement	Participation/engagement of Elders and family in school
Health and Well-being	Sense of belonging, cultural pride and identity, support, anti-racism
Curriculum	Inclusion of Indigenous perspectives at local level
Leadership	Effective communication, educational expectations, inclusion of parents

Table 16: Findings from the *Dare to Lead* Project[34]

Investigating Indigenous students' voices in a "Western educational system" (Donovan 2015, 613) in a different study, Donovan (2015) collates insights into the practices perceived as most engaging by Indigenous learners. By means of yarning circles (see Chapter IV.2.2), which allowed Aboriginal learners to "tell their stories with their own words embedding their cultural identity as part of the discussion" (ibid., 616), perspectives from 50 students were collected. The study reveals that students attributed particular importance to including cultural knowledge in the classroom, building authentic relationships, and creating Aboriginal spaces inside the school. Donovan concludes that "[b]y acknowledging Aboriginal culture through the curriculum and their teaching practices, teachers will help Aboriginal students to recognize that their culture has value within that educational space" (ibid., 623). However, he emphasizes that "teachers will need greater education about Aboriginal Australia to support the transfer of these understandings to our education system" (ibid.).

In a more recent study, Lewthwaite, Boon, Webber, and Laffin (2017) collect the viewpoints of Indigenous Australian students,

---

[34] Data retrieved from Milgate & Giles-Browne 2013.

parents, and teachers on quality classroom practices and the particular characteristics of quality teachers. Specifically, interviews with 27 Indigenous parents revealed that it is integral for teachers to understand the negative experiences in the history of First Nations education. These experiences included discrimination, prejudice, and the perceived inability to enact changes in contemporary Australian schooling. Apart from these impediments, the importance of code-switching skills is emphasized, indicating an acknowledgement of Indigenous learners as predominantly second language learners of SAE. Finally, parents desire teachers to "hold an alternative view of Aboriginal students and their community" and "schooling and teaching to affirm cultural identity and foster holistic development" (Lewthwaite et al. 2017, 85). While parents seemed focused on historical inequity, the 43 students in the study referred to classroom practices and the everyday school environment in the individual and group interviews. Thus, developing positive relationships with and holding high expectations of students, as well as clarifying learning intentions and literacy demands, constitute core characteristics of quality teachers according to the Aboriginal learners in the study.

Moreover, the importance of building cultural bridges to promote learning was also emphasized as learners "endorsed teacher attributes that showed teacher sensitivity to students' cultural backgrounds and, especially, language competencies" (ibid., 88). Finally, the interviews with 26 teachers revealed several points similar to those raised by parents and students as they also referred to the importance of catering for learners' needs, being mindful of code-switching and explicit approaches to teaching, and creating a supportive environment in which affective relationships are empowered. The study reveals, however, that "[d]espite this attention to diversity, when prompted, teachers' knowledge of specific practices to attend to such diversity were not elaborated upon to the detail students communicated" (ibid., 89). In sum, while parents, students, and teachers all identified the high value of code-switching abilities as well as of trustworthy relationships inside the classroom, parents focused predominantly on "negative experience with mainstream education as a product of their colonised history" (ibid., 91). In contrast, students did not address historical dimensions but "often expressed a desire for manifestation of 'care' from teachers" (ibid., 92). Unfortunately, the findings indicated that "teachers showed a limited awareness of the importance students and, especially, parents place on cultural inclusion and affirmation, especially in regards to promoting an educational experience that validates cultural identity" (ibid., 93). In addition, "teachers show a limited awareness of how historical and negative educational experiences continue to impinge on parent, and, subsequently, student engagement with schooling" (ibid., 93). Thus, the imperative of improving pre- and in-service teacher education is evident in the findings of Lewthwaite et al. (2017), which tie in with the conclusions in Donovan (2015).

Using the title *Two Worlds Apart* for their project, Philips and Luke (2017) investigate Indigenous student and community as well as non-Indigenous educators' perspectives on schooling in Australia. Both groups unanimously highlighted the issue "that Indigenous peoples continue to be viewed and 'treated' through the lens and language of cultural, intellectual and moral 'deficit'" (Philips & Luke 2017, 960). Moreover, the authors highlight that Indigenous students frequently find themselves in educational settings in which they are completely detached from their cultural backgrounds, and this results in learners' decreasing engagement in school. Thus, the Indigenous participants in the study advocated for expanding the "range of criteria for 'success' in schools for Indigenous students that include and transcend conventional measures (i.e., quality relationships, active participation and engagement, cultural knowledge)" (Philips & Luke 2017, 992). These findings connect with the imperative of establishing high-expectations relationships between teachers and learners (Sarra et al. 2018, 34).

In their systematic literature review entitled *Effective Teaching Practices for Aboriginal and Torres Strait Islander Students: A Review of the Literature*, Lloyd et al. (2015) discuss effective approaches for teaching and learning with Indigenous Australian students and identify system-related issues as well as core imperatives for pre-

and in-service teacher training in the Australian educational context. To start with, opinion papers in the field frequently highlight the issue of institutionalized racism and an ongoing colonialist attitude in contemporary educational discourse in Australia. Specifically, educators were criticized for frequently holding "negative conceptions of Indigenous language, logic and cognition, attitude and behaviour, culture," which constitute "impediments to student learning" (ibid., 6). Alternatively, papers providing suggestions for effective classroom practice were found to revolve around the importance of establishing strong relationships, including family and community, and harnessing cultural connections through Elders and Indigenous education workers. Moreover, these publications predominantly referred to the celebration of cultural identity, holding high expectations of Indigenous learners, to counter the prevailing deficit approach in education, as well as an awareness of cultural factors such as the concept of shame (ibid., 7). Overall, the authors detect a predominance of opinion papers alongside a lack of longitudinal, quantitative research studies evaluating the efficacy of individual teaching approaches or of programs employed. Moreover, they advocate for the adjustment of pedagogies alongside systemic matters to improve the quality of education.

The more recent literature review *Aboriginal voices: Systematic reviews of indigenous education* by Guenther, Harrison, and Burgess (2019, 210) identifies the following recurring themes for effective practices in First Nations education:

- Indigenous identity and connectedness
- Relationality between students and their communities
- Relationality to their Country and its knowledge
- Family and community engagement for effective teaching and curriculum
- Access to language/cultural programs for engagement
- Racism in schools and its effects on identities, self-esteem and success

In addition, the literature review was not able to provide an evidence-based account for the effectiveness of a specific approach to significantly improve student engagement or learning outcomes.

As such, in a similar manner to Lloyd et al. 2015, Burgess et al. (2019) also criticize the lack of research data from urban settings as well as the prevalence of case studies that are "often short-term, small scale and under-theorized, having little relevance beyond their contextual situation" (298). Hence, their comprehensive literature review reveals that "high expectations, cultural responsiveness, connectedness, relevant curriculum, engaging learning activities and inclusion of student cultural backgrounds" (Burgess et al. 2019, 298) proved to be effective teaching practices for Indigenous Australian learners. Overall, the review demonstrates a severe "mismatch between the current national curriculum, teachers' pedagogic practices, and the aspirations of Aboriginal families for their children's schooling" (Lowe et al. 2020, 2).

Derived as a central concern and desideratum from empirical studies, the improvement of pre-service teacher education constitutes a further current research dimension in Australian First Nations education. In this regard, Hughes et al. (2004, 212) emphasize that disregarding Indigenous students' diverse linguistic and cultural backgrounds is detrimental to their learning in school, yet highlight that "the renewed interest in culture has helped to emphasise the important effect of cultural influences which are characteristic of particular social groups on student behaviours and learning styles, and hence the pedagogical practices of teachers." However, as pointed out by Donovan (2015, 623) and Lewthwaite et al. (2017), among others, teachers require sound education to develop an increased awareness of Indigenous Australian perspectives, which subsequently promotes increasing responsiveness to Indigenous learners' needs.

In connection with this imperative to provide enhanced teacher training for Australian First Nations education, Daniels-Mayes (2020) explores the *racialized stories of Aboriginal deficit for pre-service teachers* in her ethnographic research project. In this study, Daniels-Mayes establishes a culturally responsive pedagogy as the most effective strategy to build teachers' confidence in relation to Indigenous perspectives and contents and in working with Indigenous students. Moreover, she pleads for the inclusion of culture and racism as significant dimensions of pre-service teacher training, claiming the following:

> [I]f teachers are to become culturally responsive educators, then they will need to analyse themselves and their own practices with regard to racism or they run the risk of perpetuating a system that benefits those affiliated with the dominant culture while continuing to disadvantage culturally marginalized students. (Daniels-Mayes 2020, 552)

Consequently, culturally responsive teachers in contemporary Australia work "towards disrupting racialised narratives borne out of two centuries of dispossessing colonisation" (Daniels-Mayes 2020, 552).

In this regard, Harrison et al. (2019) highlight the benefits of learning from, about and through Country, i.e. using Country as curriculum in their literature review. Thus, the authors advocate for "land education" as a vital factor in Indigenous pedagogy, in which Indigenous learners' identities are strengthened and schooling is decolonized through an active engagement with the past and an acknowledgment of Indigenous Australians as the original owners of the land.

Building on Harrison et al. (2019), Thorpe, Burgess, and Egan (2021), have recently investigated the impact of place-based learning courses led by Aboriginal communities on pre-service teachers' knowledge and confidence regarding Indigenous perspectives to improve teaching practice and facilitate Indigenous students' identities and learning processes. By means of surveys and yarns (see Chapter IV) the findings demonstrate that the courses achieved an increased understanding of Indigenous perspectives and elicited the development of a critical consciousness allowing teachers to reflect on their own practice. In summary, "learning by doing" was shown to be an efficient tool as all 64 pre-service teachers had a chance to listen to actual lived experiences, discover new ways of including Indigenous perspectives, and connect with First Nations communities: "through exposure to Aboriginal ways of knowing, being, and doing, opportunities to mobilise a critical consciousness became an important element of the journey" (Thorpe et al. 2021,

70). As participants revealed an enhanced understanding of the diversity of Indigenous cultures and recognized the imperative to actively include community-informed Indigenous knowledge and perspectives in their classroom practices, the authors advocate for place-based learning as a fruitful approach in teacher education.

Finally, recent research on First Nations perspectives in education has also evaluated the implementation of language and culture programs across Australian schools. Fundamentally, the establishment of such initiatives "should not be underestimated, especially when considering the complex language ecologies found within Australia" (Lowe et al. 2021, 79). Lowe et al. (2021) collect papers reporting on the efficacy of such programs in a comprehensive literature review. Overall, "providing them with the tools to renegotiate the two-world identities" (Lowe et al. 2021, 88), the programs were found to have positive effects on the development and manifestation of Indigenous Australian learners' identity, their connection with Indigenous communities, the intergenerational transmission of cultural knowledge, and school engagement. Specifically, the authors highlight the "opportunities for local knowledges to enter the mainstream classroom" (Lowe et al. 2021, 87) and that evidence derived from the studies reviewed confirms that "the acquisition of a community's own language connected students to the unique body of ancestral cultural knowledge and the epistemic mysteries of their Country" (Lowe et al. 2021, 89).

2. Objectives and Design of the Study

Despite evident efforts to address core concern areas in Australian First Nations education, such as investigating lower achievement levels, exploring effective teaching practices, improving teacher education, and implementing language and culture prograes, research in the field has tended to focus on challenges and obstacles rather than potentials. Moreover, although studies have included Indigenous perspectives on quality education and effective teaching practice, they have frequently been limited to case studies investigating approaches adopted at certain schools, or have provided insights from rather specific contexts. With the exception of

Philips and Luke (2017), previous projects have rarely captured, contrasted, and investigated perspectives and experiences of different stakeholders in First Nations education in a single study. Moreover, as most Indigenous Australian students learn SAE as a second language or dialect (see Chapter III.3.1), research projects have so far rarely investigated the English language learning component in First Nations education.

Consequently, the objective of this research project was to investigate the role of Australian First Nations' language and culture in their learning at school. Moreover, besides exploring dimensions that present a challenge, it was also necessary to identify the possibilities of incorporating Indigenous Australian perspectives in the classroom, so as to derive recommendations and incentives for teaching practice in multicultural classrooms in different contexts. Consolidating the opinions and experiences of different experts in education, including teachers, Aboriginal and Islander education workers, principals, and university lecturers, profound insights into the learning context of Indigenous Australian students were gained. The underlying research questions of this study read as follows:

RQ1: *Which language-related factors do experienced educators perceive to impact Indigenous Australian students' learning in school?*

RQ2: *Which culture-related factors do experienced educators perceive to impact Indigenous Australian students' learning in school?*

RQ3: *Which challenges exist in teaching and learning with Indigenous Australian students according to experienced educators?*

RQ4: *How can Indigenous Australian students' home language and culture be incorporated in teaching materials and methodology according to experienced educators?*

Figure 11: Research Questions

Due to their close relation to the Indigenous pedagogy of storytelling (see Chapter IV.2.2), semi-guided interviews (Brinkman & Kvale 2015, 5) were chosen as valuable research instruments, given the context and objectives of the study. According to Seidman (2013, 9), "[a]t the root of in-depth interviewing is an interest in understanding the lived experience of other people and the meaning they make of that experience." Hence, insights into the practices, opinions, and experiences of both Indigenous as well as non-Indigenous participants were gained in the study. In order to provide a practical example of how Indigenous perspectives can be included in teaching materials and methodology, an analysis of the *Honey Ant Readers* textbook series (James 2015a), written and published by Australian linguist Margaret James, constitutes an additional part of the research project.

In total, the findings of this study contribute to research on Indigenous perspectives in multicultural classrooms and should assist and educate teachers in regards to the essential consideration of learners' cultural diversity.

2.1 Procedure

The research design of the guided interview demanded certain steps in its organization and realization, including the process of constructing the interview form, transcribing the oral data, coding the transcripts, and analyzing the coded material. These stages are outlined in the following sections.

2.1.1 *Constructing the Interview Form*

The designed interview form (see Appendix) builds on the research questions listed above and underwent several stages of piloting, testing, revising, and editing in which the questions were rephrased and clarified and the structure of the interview was adapted. Generally, the interview questions were phrased and structured in accordance with guidelines obtained from Brinkmann and Kvale (2015), Seidman (2013) and King and Horrocks (2010). The questions reveal an internal structure evolving from specific to more general so as to prevent interviewees from repetition and encourage elaboration of previous answers, generating a broader view on the topic.

As can be seen in the Appendix, the final version of the interview form used in the project consists of three main sections: language, culture, and challenges. Hence, part A looks at the role of Indigenous students' home language and asks the participants to assess the significance of its consideration and incorporation in school. Similarly, part B investigates the importance of learners' home culture. In addition, both parts also ask for the significance of students' linguistic and cultural backgrounds for their English language learning. Moreover, both sections contain questions encouraging participants to share strategies and recommendations for including Indigenous Australian learners' backgrounds in teaching materials and methodology. Possible challenges are then discussed in the concluding part C.

2.1.2 Transcribing the Interview Data

In order to analyze the information gathered in the interviews, the oral data had to be converted into written form, i.e. transcribed, in a way that adequately illustrated the original conversation. Since content rather than linguistic facets in relation to participants' answers were of interest for this research project, a simple transcription format was chosen, adopting a slight variation of the model presented by Dresing and Pehl (2015, 21–25). In order for the transcripts to accurately express the underlying orality of the acquired information, the following symbols were used (see Table 17).

Sign	Meaning
(.)	Short pause (< 5 seconds)
(..)	Pause (5–10 seconds)
(...)	Long pause (> 10 seconds)
/	Unfinished sentence, truncation
CAPITAL	Emphasis
[laughs]	Paralinguistic feature, comment or additional information
xxx	Deletion for reasons of anonymity or privacy
?	Unintelligible section
'...'	Quoting somebody
[...]	Omission

Table 17: Conventions for Transcriptions[35]

Moreover, certain aspects were omitted in the course of transcribing the interview data. Table 18 provides an overview of what was transcribed and what was omitted in the final transcripts:

Transcribed	Omitted
Repetitions used for emphasis or as a stylistic device	Repetitions without emphasis or new information and redundancies
Mhm if it is the only answer; either affirmative or negative	Backchanneling to signal understanding, e.g. mhm, yeah
Translating dialects into Standard Australian English; exception: gonna was not changed into its formal equivalent	Information that is not significant for the study or unrelated to the field of research
Truncated "whole" half-sentences	Truncated, unfinished trains of thought
Pauses	False starts and slips
Emphasis on certain words or phases	

Table 18: Transcribed and Omitted Information[36]

In addition to the conventions above, further reasons for omitting particular parts of the interview in the transcriptions include overly

---

[35] Modified from Dresing & Pehl 2015, 21–25.
[36] Modified from Dresing & Pehl 2015, 21–25.

personal information and elaborations that were unrelated or irrelevant to the field of research. The original duration of the interviews as well as the final amount of time used for the transcriptions is listed in Table 19.

Participant number	Original time [hrs:min:sec]	Time Transcribed [hrs:min:sec]	Time not transcribed [hrs:min:sec]	Value transcribed
P1	00:43:03	00:36:48	00:06:15	85%
P2	00:27:45	00:25:49	00:01:56	93%
P3	00:30:37	00:30:17	00:00:20	99%
P4	00:47:54	00:43:56	00:03:58	92%
P5	00:37:40	00:37:13	00:00:27	99%
P6	01:21:48	01:05:12	00:16:36	80%
P7	00:46:13	00:45:01	00:01:12	97%
P8	00:34:07	00:33:39	00:00:28	99%
P9	00:45:17	00:43:29	00:01:48	96%
P10	00:35:43	00:34:56	00:00:47	98%
P11	00:27:52	00:27:45	00:00:07	100%
Mean	00:41:38	00:38:33	00:03:05	93%

Table 19: Duration of Interviews[37]

2.1.3 Coding the Transcripts

Following the transcription of the oral data, the three steps in the subsequent meaning-focused interview analysis are coding, condensation, and interpretation (Brinkmann & Kvale 2015, 223). In the study, Mayring's summarizing qualitative content analysis based on an inductive formation of categories was applied. A main goal of this approach is to systematically condense transcribed data through the application of a series of reduction processes and the generation of a coding scheme (Mayring 2015, 49), which captures the essence of the interviews so that hypotheses and theories can be formulated subsequently (Brinkmann & Kvale 2015, 227). In alignment with Mayring's approach, a coding scheme was developed in

---

[37] To preserve their anonymity, the eleven participants are referenced as P1, P2, etc.

a predominantly inductive manner. Fundamentally, the interview questions formed the basis for the initial coding scheme. Throughout the proofreading process, and while rereading the transcripts, salient aspects and ideas were either allotted to the existing categories or generated new codes. The resulting coding scheme, which will be presented in section 3, formed the starting point for the ensuing evaluation and interpretation.

2.2 Sample

With regards to the field and objectives of the study, several groups of people could be considered experts. Being directly involved in the teaching and learning process, Aboriginal students, present and past, as well as future students, can clearly be regarded as experts in their own learning. Naturally, parents contribute a further perspective, as they themselves experienced a certain type of education and now witness their children's situation in school. For this study, the perspective of educators was chosen due to their experience and their ability to actively cause change in schools.

Furthermore, since the linguistic and cultural background, as well as the learning context of Indigenous Australian students can be very multifaceted, a greater variation among the interviewees and hence a broader perspective was achieved by including participants working in different fields of education. Thus, the opinions and experiences of primary and secondary school teachers, teaching assistants, principals, and university professors were included in the research. Moreover, educators at government schools, private schools, and Indigenous schools were interviewed. Finally, as the research investigates Indigenous students' learning in school, the study naturally aims at emphasizing Indigenous voices.

Consequently, the various perspectives represented by the selected experts in education are illustrated in Figure 12.

Research Study 119

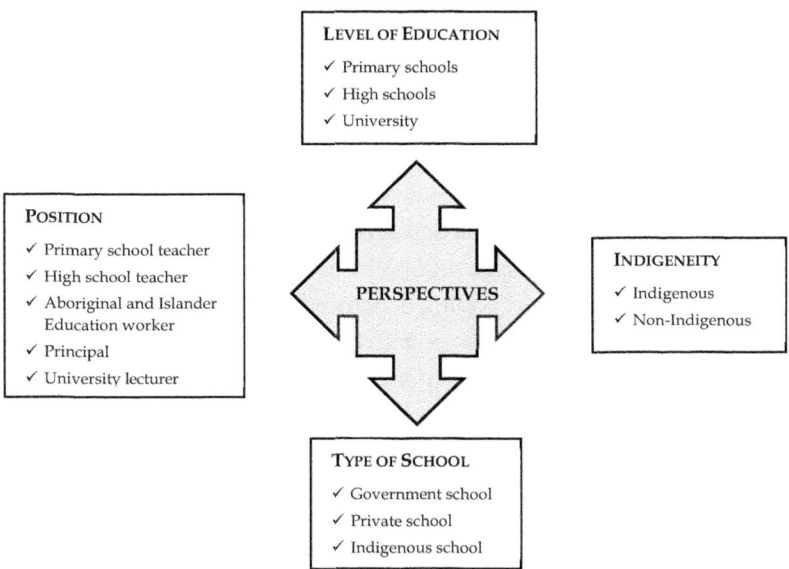

Figure 12: Perspectives represented by the Sample

With these specifications, the final sample consisted of the following participants (Table 20):

Participant	Level & Type of School	Position	Indigeneity
P1	Government Primary School	Teacher	Non-Indigenous
P2	University	Lecturer	Indigenous
P3	Aboriginal Primary School	Teacher	Indigenous
P4	Aboriginal High School	Principal	Indigenous
P5	Private High School	Teacher	Non-Indigenous
P6	University	Lecturer	Indigenous
P7	Government High School	Aboriginal and Islander Education Worker	Indigenous
P8	Government High School	Aboriginal and Islander Education Worker	Indigenous
P9	Government High School	Teacher	Non-Indigenous
P10	Aboriginal Primary School	Teacher	Indigenous
P11	Private High School	Aboriginal and Islander Education Worker	Non-Indigenous

Table 20: Characteristics of the Sample[38]

---

[38] Modified from Peskoller 2019, 200.

In order to guarantee confidentiality and protection of identity, the interviewees are only referred to by their position, region, Indigeneity, or type and level of educational institution in this book.

3. Findings

In this section, the results of the research study are presented. First, the role of Indigenous languages and cultures in learning is discussed on the basis of the generated coding schemes as well as frequency analyses for the respective categories. Subsequently, challenges in Indigenous education identified by the participants in the study are explored. Finally, the importance of and suggestions for incorporating Indigenous perspectives in classroom discourse are outlined.

3.1 The Role of Indigenous Languages

The interview study revealed a variety of factors in connection with the influence of Indigenous Australian students' linguistic heritage on their learning, resulting in the following multifaceted coding scheme:

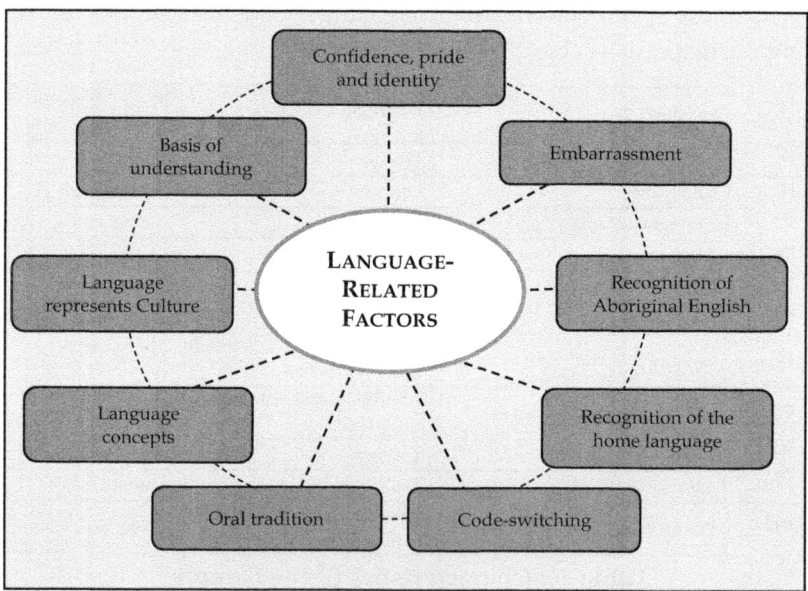

Figure 13:
Language-related Factors Identified in the Interview Data

As can be seen in Figure 13, nine major categories in connection with the role of Indigenous Australian students' home languages in their learning in school were identified. At this stage, it is important to note that the arrangement of the categories is not indicative of their respective relevance. The figure intends to provide an overview and express the interconnectedness of the identified codes. These are discussed and represented in a combined manner below.

3.1.1 Pride vs. Embarrassment

The majority of interviews revealed that the home language is "a source of pride for Aboriginal children" (P1) and is vital for their confidence, well-being, and sense of identity. In this regard, P2 indicated the following:

> I think when Aboriginal students are learning language, their first language again or another [Aboriginal] language, it makes them feel strong, it builds their self-esteem, it builds their well-being. And I know from my aunties that could still speak languages they were so proud to be able to have language spoken again and to teach it to young children and young children feeling excited about having this so (.) it's very special having access to this.

Being a teacher at a school where a traditional Aboriginal language is taught to all children, P7 argued that "it gives them pride in their own culture to know that not just them, everybody else, all their peers are learning THEIR language (.) and the kids love it." On the contrary, Aboriginal students also often experience a feeling of embarrassment or inferiority in school due to their home language since "correcting and making students feel they're wrong tends to (.) impact on their self-esteem, which then impacts on their learning" (P7). In this sense, the Aboriginal university lecturer stated that "it's not that our kids don't know how to learn, it's how it's taught, how people are approached around language and how people are made to feel inferior because they speak language" (P2).

The highlighted topic of students' linguistic heritage potentially causing both feelings of pride and embarrassment links with the imperative for an enhanced appreciation of Indigenous Australian students' home languages in school, which constitutes a further category in the coding scheme.

3.1.2 Recognition of Linguistic Heritage

The majority of participants in the study expressed the need for an intensified awareness of learners' linguistic heritage in school. Despite the recognition of Aboriginal English as a distinct variety and dialect of SAE (Eades 2013), P6 observed that

> teachers have, sort of, treated Aboriginal English as a second-rate language, as a poor version of English or, you know, a rough version of English. [...] So a lot of Aboriginal kids drop out or don't do well, because they see the teacher thinks they can't speak properly.

Hence, an Aboriginal and Islander education worker indicated that if "Aboriginal English is not put down but (.) accepted and what they have to offer rather than how they offer it is the most important thing, then that student will thrive, their confidence will build" (P7). Looking at the recognition of the home language, i.e. traditional Aboriginal languages and AE, more broadly, it was generally emphasized in the interviews that "considering that they [students] are learning English as another language is HUGELY important" (P11). Adding to this, a high school teacher stated that what is essential is

> an understanding that English is always a second language for them. Even if their mother tongue is English, they are always aware that that's another language. So with some understanding of their own language (.) it just evens, my opinion is it evens the balance up.

Thus, the home language constitutes the basis of understanding for Aboriginal students. P5 indicated that "obviously your home language is the language that you understand things through and even if you are speaking a different language, a second language, and that, moving back through your original language, that's where your understanding comes from."

3.1.3 Orality of Indigenous Languages

In connection with the recognition of students' home languages, all interviewees invariably highlighted that Indigenous languages originally were and continue to be characterized by their oral nature. For instance, P3 claimed that "in the Indigenous context they're often coming from a background of no print literacy, a lot of oral literacy, they might speak four or five languages in the desert, [...] but not print literacy." Consequently, "the reading and writing skills are often a long way behind" (P9). Due to the orality of traditional languages, participants expressed the need to provide additional support for fostering Indigenous Australian students' reading and writing skills so that "as a teacher, responsibility lies with trying to fill that void and bring up their written skills so their communication is compatible with their intellect and their capacity to communicate that" (P5). In this context, educators in the study frequently referred to the concept of code-switching, which emerged as a distinct category.

3.1.4 Code-switching

In the context of the Australian school system, with "English being the basis of everything that we're doing" (P5), the development of code-switching abilities, referring to the conscious switch between the students' home language and SAE, was identified as a vital basis for the predominantly multilingual Indigenous Australian learners. In this regard, P8 observed: "What we're seeing is students who are successful are able to (.) communicate using their home style but also communicate using the formal English that we use in schools. So, they're able to step from one into the other." Moreover, connecting code-switching to the aforementioned categories, the principal of an Indigenous school in the NT shared:

> For us the focus is [...] on developing an understanding of Standard Australian English and how to code-switch between the two, Aboriginal English and Standard English, and also to develop the skills with reading, which often the students do not have, and also writing skills, both in Aboriginal English and Standard English. (P4)

3.1.5 Language Concepts and Worldview

Touching on several aforementioned factors such as orality, several language concepts that potentially influence Indigenous Australian students' learning exist since "they're not just translating, they're learning new concepts as well as the language" (P11). Specifically, certain vocabulary and terminology frequently render translations between languages impossible, hampering understanding and impeding learning processes as a consequence (P6). To exemplify this reality often faced by Indigenous students, P11 explained that in some traditional languages

> they might have numbers up to ten and then beyond ten you just have many. So when they come to our language, they're not just learning a new language for a number, a new number in the language, they're learning that there is a number, there is a specific number for many.

Moreover, *Language represents Culture* formed an additional code alluding to the fact that language constitutes a medium through which cultural dimensions are expressed. The majority of participants showed strong agreement that "language affects your worldview and sort of moulds your worldview so […] depending on the students' exposure to this language and concepts that sort of influences how they see the world" (P4). Linking to this, the principal of an Indigenous school in the NT added that in textbooks,

> you might have a unit entirely to do with seasons but clearly, up here, there aren't four season words, there are twelve or fifteen different words for seasons. So I think, sometimes (.) there is no easy way just to translate between them because the whole worldview behind it is wrapped up in the language. (P4)

3.2 The Role of Indigenous Cultures

Having discussed different aspects relating to the home language, the focus is now on identifying facets of Indigenous Australian students' home culture that affect their learning in school. The categories were again generated inductively by determining major themes in the participants' shared viewpoints and experiences, which resulted in the following coding scheme (Figure 14):

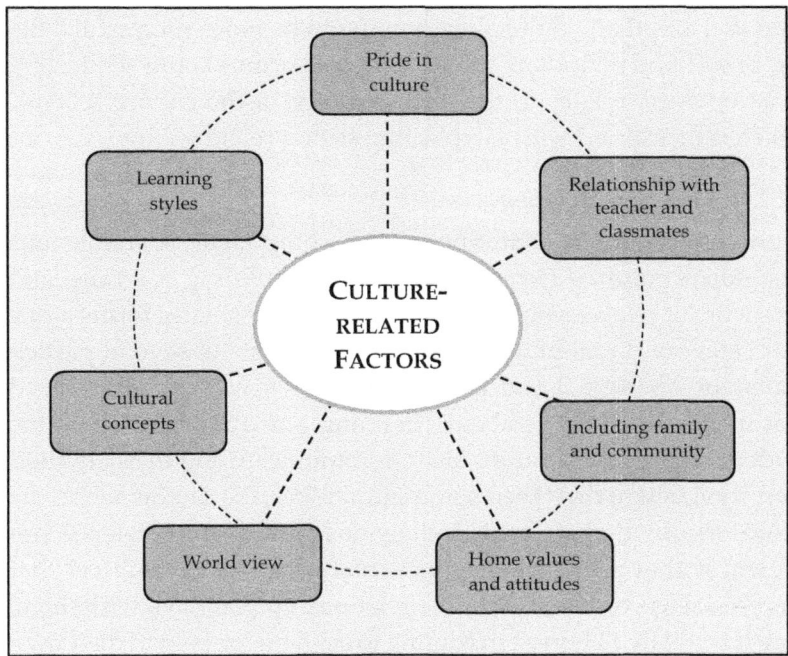

Figure 14:
Culture-related Factors Identified in the Interview Data

As before, the categories will be discussed and represented in a combined manner below.

3.2.1 Pride in Culture

This first category in the coding scheme denotes that students feel proud and confident about their cultural identity and acknowledge the value of their home culture. An Aboriginal and Islander education worker at a high school in NSW observed the following in relation to the consideration of Indigenous cultures in school:

> What it means to an Indigenous person is that their culture and their side and their tradition is being respected and that it has use, that it has worth. It makes them proud, it makes them want to learn and engage in learning more, it improves their attendance and overall it improves their success at school. (P8)

In a similar manner, P10 emphasized that "if you are self-assured and if you know that you're accepted and if you know that you're who you are, then you're always going to be more successful." Being proud and confident about one's background, and the feeling of acceptance, relates to the next category of the coding scheme, which is concerned with establishing strong relationships.

3.2.2 Relationship Building

With connections constituting a vital component of Indigenous Australian cultures (see Chapter IV.2.1), building a strong and trustworthy relationship with teachers and classmates forms a further category. In alignment with the statements of several participants, an Aboriginal and Islander education worker emphasized that in-class learning is about "building a relationship where the student feels really comfortable to communicate and to ask in their own way, where they need some extra help" (P5). In this sense, the educator added that "with Indigenous kids […] experience has shown, if they feel that they can trust you and if they feel that there's a sense of integrity in the relationship you have with them, they'll be really (.) honest in coming to ask you for help in their own way" (P5). Building on this argument, the Indigenous university lecturer claimed that, as a teacher, "if you don't know how to relate to your students, if you don't know how to build relationships with them and their families, and then build that into your teaching and learning […] you'll be useless" (P6).

3.2.3 Family and Community Involvement

Building strong and trustworthy relationships is closely linked to the participants' addressed need to include family and community in educational contexts. According to an Aboriginal and Islander education worker, this entails "having Elders and community people come into the school and be a part of their learning. We know how much of a difference that makes" (P7). The educator from an Indigenous primary school emphasized that, for teaching, "you need to ensure that you are relating with the actual people in that culture, you need to consult the Elders of the area and you need to make sure that they are involved to make it [learning] genuine" (P10). Hence, including family and community members in the teaching and learning process "impacts on the children's experience at school, because if they don't any longer have a really negative (.) experience about this school in particular then it might flow on to their kids and grandchildren" (P7).

Alongside the dimension of family and community involvement, teachers' mindfulness of students' home values, attitudes towards education, and worldviews were deemed essential and are discussed under the next heading.

3.2.4 Home Values and Worldview

Several participants accentuated aspects in connection with Aboriginal Australian students' worldview and home values as decisive factors for successful learning. In this regard, an Aboriginal and Islander education worker outlined the following:

> A particular culture's view of an attitude of learning has a big impact. I think there's only so much a school can do in some ways if at home/ I think at home is where it's gonna come from the desire for an education. In some cultures that is incredibly valued and other cultures (.) not as much and that makes a huge impact on how much a child puts in when they're in the classroom. (P11)

Moreover, several participants addressed aspects in connection with Indigenous Australian learners' worldviews as a contributing factor for learning. P6, for instance, indicated that "culture teaches you certain ways to behave and act and (.) even interpret the world. So, you interpret the world through your own cultural lens." In a similar manner, P3 stated that "your background experience influences everything that you do, it influences the way you view the world, it influences the way you react to something." Furthermore, P4, among other interviewees, suggested that there was the ensuing need for teachers "to constantly take into account the worldview that the students are coming from in how they learn, whether that's English or any topic."

3.2.5 Cultural Concepts and Learning Styles

A further facet of Indigenous Australian students' cultural backgrounds that participants identified as essential relates to differing Indigenous and non-Indigenous cultural concepts. For instance, educators should be aware of the fact that there are certain differences "in terms of parenting and family. A lot of Indigenous kids are given a lot more autonomy at a younger age than a Western family might do" (P4). Moreover, the participant highlighted that "the kids are encouraged to make choices or make decisions (.) as opposed to being protected or overprotected" (P4). Adding to this, another interviewee shared that "sitting at a desk, picking up a pen, pulling in your chair, obeying rules is completely foreign because in a lot of their cultures […] children are not told what to do, the children dictate (.) what they want to do when they're very young" (P3). A further aspect relating to cultural concepts was addressed by the university lecturer: "What we tend to find with Aboriginal kids is (.) please and thank you for instance aren't necessarily words that are used […] because there's a sort of in-built sense of reciprocity in anything they do" (P6). Also, certain aspects highlighted in the interviews strongly relate to the concept of shame in Aboriginal cultures (see Chapter IV.2.3).

Finally, tendencies in learning styles relevant for Indigenous Australian students were discussed by some participants. The principal of an Indigenous school stated that "a lot from their way of learning is watch, observe, gain competency and then do" (P4). Therefore, their school in the NT pursues the "idea of gradually withdrawing the teacher's input as opposed to […] that sort of inquiry-based learning. […] We heavily place a lot more presence on (.) trial and error or finding things out that way as opposed to (.) wanting to have expert advice passed over" (P4). Finally, an Aboriginal and Islander education worker observed that

> Aboriginal students tend to a) like and b) excel at practical subjects. That's because Aboriginal people, historically, have learnt that way. It's the practical things they learn by doing. Rarely would you be sat and spoken/ talked to in the learning process, you would be shown how. And I know that's typical for Indigenous cultures all over the world. (P7)

3.3 Frequency Analyses of Language and Culture Categories

Several dimensions in relation to Indigenous Australian students' home language and culture relevant for their learning in school were identified by means of the guided interviews. These factors created the multitude of categories resulting in the two coding schemes presented in the previous sections. In order to provide an additional perspective on the assigned relevance of codes, the categories are assembled in descending order of frequency in the following bar chart. In Figure 16, the categories for language and culture are presented collectively with an applied differentiation in color. If addressed in the interview, an individual category was counted once per participant regardless of its frequency within the interview. Therefore, a code can attain the maximum value of eleven in the following figure:

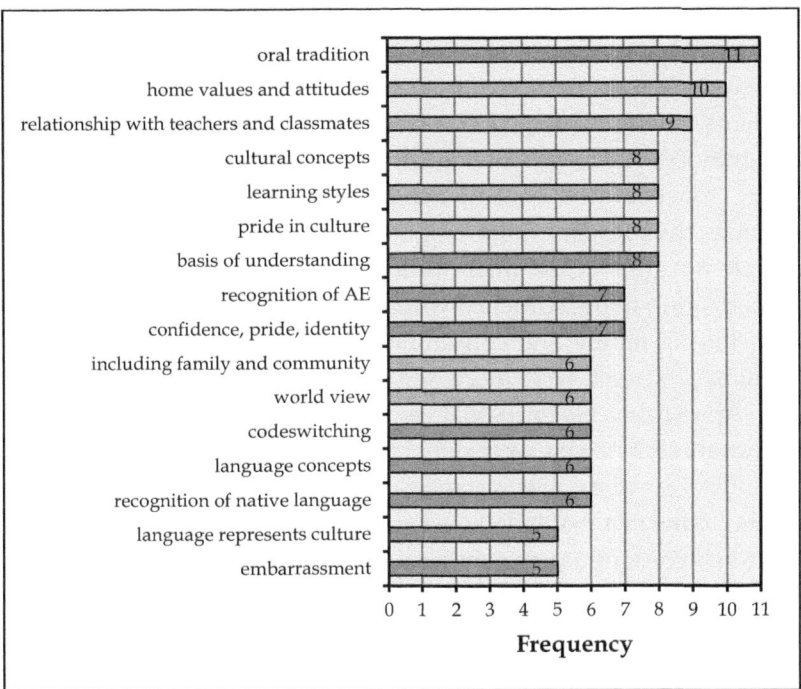

Figure 15: Frequency of Codes: Language and Culture

As can be seen from the chart, all participants mentioned aspects relating to the oral tradition of Indigenous languages as decisive for student learning. Looking particularly at learners' home culture, ten of the eleven educators highlighted the significance of home values and the family or community attitudes towards learning, schooling, and the English language. Moreover, the importance of strong relationships with teachers and among classmates was extensively addressed throughout the interviews. Specifically, eight of the eleven participants advocate for teachers' thorough consideration that students' home language constitutes the foundation of their understanding and learning.

According to several interviewees, both the home language and culture form an essential source of pride for Indigenous Australian students, which can result in an empowered sense of identity and increased confidence. Aspects connected to Indigenous students' preferred learning styles that educators should consider to ensure successful learning were also suggested by most experts. Moreover, roughly half of the participants identified the acknowledgment of the students' home language as vital for their learning, considering the recognition of Aboriginal English as particularly important. Language concepts and code-switching were further categories connected to the students' home language addressed by about half of the sample throughout the interviews. On the other hand, cultural aspects relating to the students' worldview, as well as the significance of including family and community members in the teaching and learning processes, were discussed by six of the eleven interviewees.

Apart from categories that were addressed by the majority of the educators, some codes were only referred to by a few participants in the interview study. For instance, only five participants' statements related to the fact that language represents students' home culture or that the home language can be a cause of embarrassment for students in school. Interestingly, all codes, including those with the fewest denominations, were addressed by almost half of the educators. In addition, the different frequencies of the categories might be indicative of their respective significance in the school context.

Supplementing Figure 15 by looking at the participants' allocations of codes individually, Figure 16 provides a further perspective on the obtained data. The size of the circles in the chart indicates the amount of coding within the interviews, wherein particularly frequently or relatively rarely used categories in an interview are visualized.

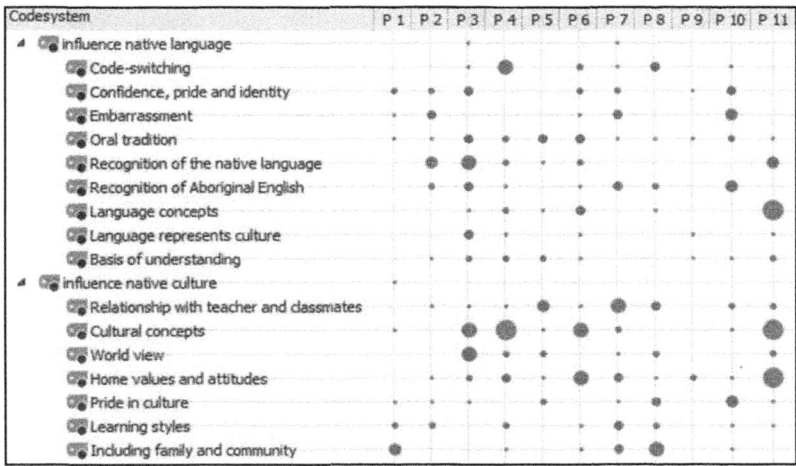

Figure 16: Code-Matrix-Browser: Language and Culture[39]

Initially it can be seen in the figure above that, even though categories such as code-switching or language concepts were only named by half of the interviewees, the principal of an Indigenous school and an Aboriginal and Islander education worker elaborated on them extensively. Furthermore, the recognition of the home language was also discussed in greater detail by certain interviewees. On the contrary, despite the fact that the oral tradition of Indigenous languages was addressed by all experts, none of them notably expanded on this topic.

Looking at the influence of the home culture, categories that were explored in particular depth by certain participants include cultural concepts, the relationship with the teacher and classmates, and the students' worldview. Four Indigenous participants highlighted the importance of the recognition of home languages in the interviews, with half of them additionally emphasizing the aspect of embarrassment or the significance of code-switching ability. Moreover, the categories expanded on the most by the Indigenous interviewees concerned the role of the home culture for learning, and included the relationship with teacher and classmates, Indigenous learning styles, and home values and attitudes. These aspects

---

[39] Image generated with MAXQDA12.

were also among the most frequently addressed categories throughout all the interviews.

3.4 Challenges in Indigenous Education

Having discussed the role and importance of Indigenous Australian students' home language and culture for their learning, the focus shall now turn to identifying the existing challenges Indigenous students face in the Australian school system. While several of the previously defined codes already alluded to some of these, the emerging code system is depicted in Figure 17:

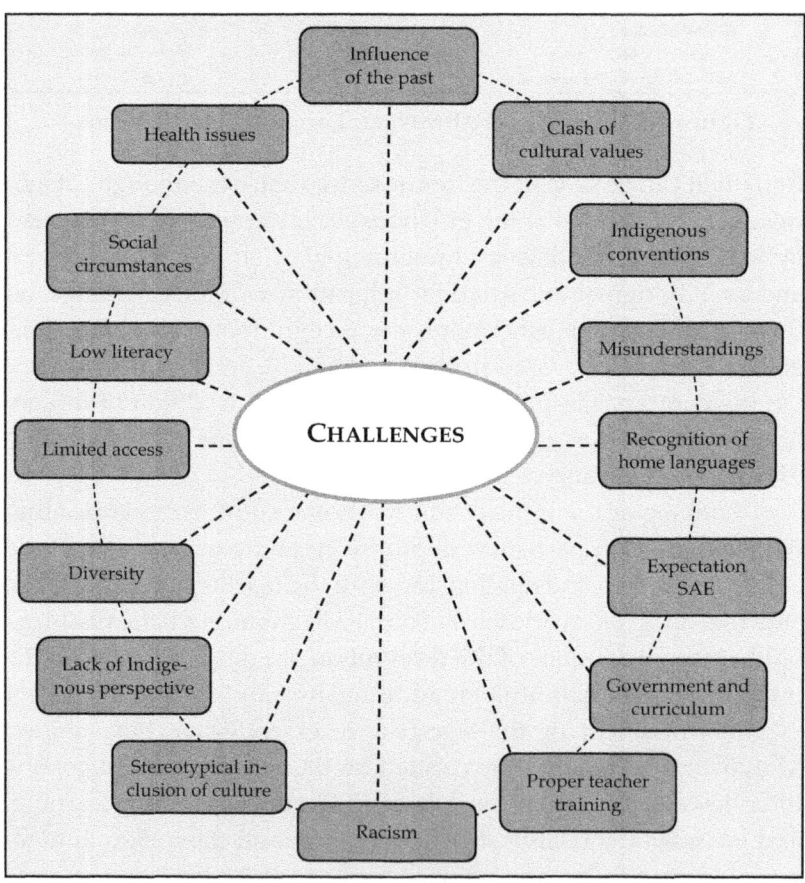

Figure 17: Challenges Identified in the Interview Data

The identified categories are presented in a combined manner and in the order that appeared most logical and comprehensible. As before, the depiction and order of the presentation of the codes does not correlate to their respective relevance.

3.4.1 Historical Burden

A first challenge identified by participants in the study is the *influence of the past*, referring to aspects that relate past events to present attitudes or mindsets. One factor that experts in First Nations education address relates to the loss of Indigenous Australian languages. An Aboriginal and Islander education worker stated the following in this context:

> In this school, we're only just starting to bring the home languages back, it's been lost for quite a while and for a long time because of government policies and people weren't allowed to practice their customs and their language [...] There was always that fear that if we practiced our culture and our language that they would be taken away. (P8)

In connection with the English language and the feelings it might provoke in learners, P3 argued that "when the English first arrived, they came in as conquerors of their land and basically stole a lot of their languages. So, there is, I am sure, an underlying kind of resentment towards the language."

3.4.2 Culture-related Differences

In addition to language-related factors, Australia's colonial past also caused a clash of cultural values in Australian society, as indicated by participants in the study. A high school teacher exemplified this by observing that in Indigenous cultures "it's that sense of all working together as one community, as one family, as one unity. The culture of our school is about achieving your best for yourself. So you've got a clash of cultures immediately" (P5). Referring to this comment and connecting with the dimension of learning styles and cultural concepts (see section 3.2), P6 emphasized that Indigenous learners "tend to be more collaborative rather than competitive. They tend to wanna work as a group, not work as an individual. And, of course, our school system is set up on the individual competition and achievement."

Another challenging category generated by means of the explorative study relates to Indigenous conventions. As illustrated by P3, many Aboriginal communities would, for instance, not want to have someone from a different language group teach their language or have their language taught off-country, i.e. not on the land it was traditionally spoken on. This can understandably complicate possibilities for learners to access their home language. Joining the previous codes, a further category in connection with culture-related differences is that of misunderstandings. In order to exemplify this dimension, P3 outlined that

> you've got that problem for the students where they think that the teacher is saying one thing and the teacher thinks that they're saying one thing and they're actually completely misunderstanding one another. There are a lot of cultural things such as an Aboriginal person would generally try and please you so they would try and they will tend to say what it is they think you want to hear rather than what they think the correct answer is. […] So some of those unseen differences are the ones that cause the most misunderstandings.

3.4.3 Lack of Awareness and Recognition

Linked to the dimensions addressed in section 3.1, teachers' recognition of home languages was identified as a vital element for learning outcomes and, equally, as a challenge in teaching practice. In this context, an important point, made by the participants, relates to the inequality in recognition of home languages of students coming from different linguistic backgrounds. To be exact, the status of a second language learner is "acknowledged for other language speakers but for Aboriginal students it's not. And just, you know, in hospitals, there aren't interpreter services for Aboriginal languages even though there's interpreter services for Mandarin" (P2). Hence, Indigenous Australian students are frequently assumed to be proficient speakers of SAE even though for the majority of them SAE constitutes a second language or dialect (see Chapter III.3.1), which relates to a further code: *expectation SAE*. In connection with the realities faced by Indigenous learners making schooling difficult for them, P3 shared:

> It's MUCH more difficult for them than if you were speaking Polish or French where it's really clear that you've come in as a second language learner. So they don't get that second language support (.) and because it's

similar (.) when they write in Aboriginal English it can be presumed that they're writing in Standard English but making grammatical mistakes but it's not that at all. [...] It's actually incredibly different, structurally, culturally, the culture embedded in the language is completely different to Standard English so, in a way those students have a very difficult time because it's just presumed that they are (.) speaking English but they're not speaking it in the standardised version but in fact, they're speaking something completely different.

3.4.4 Systemic Shortcomings in Education

A further cluster that emerged in participants' discussions refers to shortcomings in education. Connecting expectation SAE to the further code of government and curriculum, P4 stated that "a lot of the national curriculum and the benchmarks presume that Standard Australian English is their first language. So automatically, the kids are in deficit basically, because they're learning it often as a second or third language or dialect." In connection with this aspect, the issue of low literacy levels among most Indigenous Australian learners ties in with the previous categories. As P3 shared,

> the problem is that a lot of languages don't have many people who can read or write that language so that's your first hurdle. Really there are very, very few people who can translate and some of the languages you would have absolutely nobody who could properly write other than a non-Indigenous linguist.

Looking at government policies, the lack of proper teacher training was also addressed by the participants. For instance, the Indigenous university lecturer highlighted that, put in a classroom with Indigenous students right after finishing their teaching degree, "people weren't ready, prepared or didn't know what they were walking into. And they didn't have the skills to be (.) cross-cultural and that's really what is needed to teach" (P2). The interviewee also condensed links between the aforementioned formalities in the education system and the category of *racism* and clarified that the main challenges were

> teaching, the curriculum, the current curriculum, the level of racism and systemic racism. It's institutional, systemic and personal (.) and that causes harm. Racism actually makes people sick and discrimination actually impacts on learning. And so, if you're in an environment where you're having racism, you're not gonna want to learn.

3.4.5 Lack or Stereotypical Inclusion of Culture

The *stereotypical inclusion of home culture* can constitute a further impediment in teaching and learning with Indigenous Australian students. In some schools, P10 observed that "the culture becomes very stereotypical. Everyone will do the standard dot paintings or Christine Anu song. And whilst that's very valid, I think that you need to ensure that you are relating with the actual people in that culture." Moreover, a clear lack of Indigenous perspectives was identified in most subjects. For instance, "a lot of (.) teaching materials and text materials don't have [...] Aboriginal characters" (P4). According to the experts in education, reasons for this prevalent absence of Indigenous dimensions in class could be attributed to the great linguistic and cultural diversity among Indigenous students. P5 clarifies that with Indigenous Australian learners "[w]e're not talking about one language, we're talking about hundreds of languages and (.) we're not talking about a school that's drawing students from the same language groups, from the same area." The primary school teacher added that "even in one town you can have two, three or more different dialects from different cultural backgrounds. [...] Unless you have someone teaching them that comes from that exact background, then it's always going to be different" (P10).

Moreover, progressing from the shortcomings within the classroom, Indigenous learners also largely experience a lack of cultural connections outside of school since they have only *limited access* and connection to their home languages and cultural heritage. While P5 stated that a "lot of Australian Indigenous students don't have a direct connection to their language because so many of their languages have been lost over time," a high school teacher added that also "some of them are quite disconnected from their culture" (P9).

3.4.6 Socio-economic and Health Parameters

This final section discusses addressed challenges in connection with socio-economic and health-related parameters. The category of *social circumstances* implies that, in school, "[y]ou have Aboriginal kids who come from lower socioeconomic groups [and] again that's an issue of low literacy" (P9). A university lecturer highlighted that "still most Aboriginal families live in poverty or some form of often multiple disadvantage. It's very hard to focus on your school work if you're hungry or, if you don't have a (.) desk to do your homework at" (P6). Such conditions can naturally result in *health issues* constituting the final category of challenges. The Aboriginal university lecturer emphasized that "we're the sickest people in this country. [...] We die twenty years, or ten to twenty years earlier than the non-Indigenous population so [...] we're sicker and we die earlier" (P2).

3.5 Frequency Analyses of Challenge Categories

Having identified sixteen different yet interrelated challenges in connection with teaching and learning with Indigenous students, the following bar chart visualizes the codes in decreasing order of frequency. Counting a category, if addressed, once per participant, the maximum value to be acquired per category is eleven.

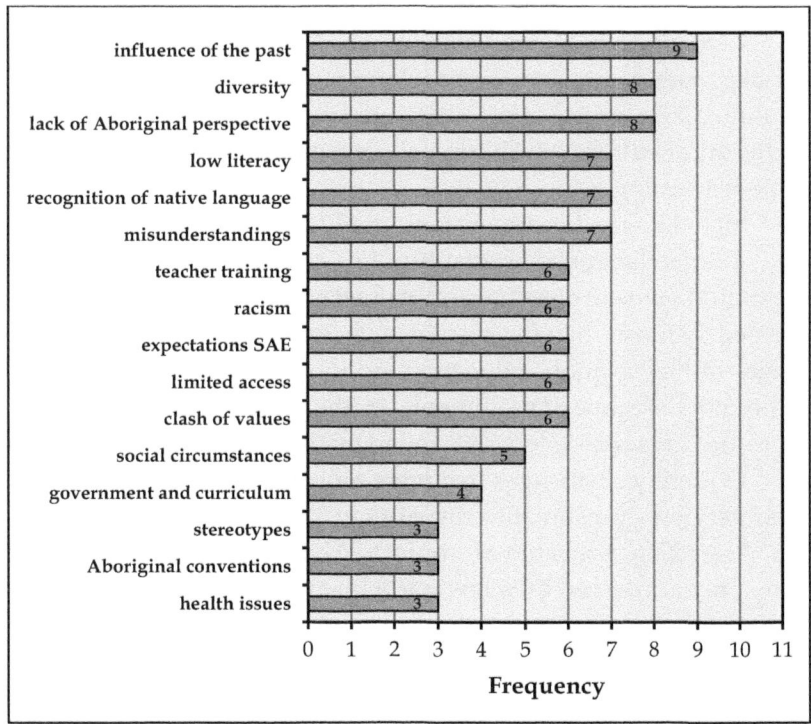

Figure 18: Frequency of Codes: Challenges

As can be seen in Figure 18, nine of the eleven participants addressed aspects relating to past events and policies as impeding learning processes in school. A lack of appropriate teaching resources for Indigenous Australian students depicting their worldviews and interests, as well as the great diversity of home languages and cultures in Indigenous Australia, constitute further major challenges that eight experts referred to. Several interviewees identified misunderstandings between the teacher and student or among classmates as problems that can be attributed to linguistic and cultural backgrounds. The recognition of the learners' linguistic heritage and their prevalently low literacy levels constitute additional challenges in Australian classrooms. Six of the eleven participants also highlighted the limited access to home languages, the predominant expectation for Aboriginal students to be proficient in SAE, and the lack of proper teacher training. Another recurring theme throughout several interviews was institutionalized racism.

Categories that were mentioned by fewer participants include social circumstances or policies relating to the government and curriculum. Only three experts elaborated on health, the stereotypical inclusion of culture or Aboriginal conventions as aspects that can impede learning.

Interestingly, for dimensions identified in connection with the role of home language and culture for learning (see section 3.3), a maximum value of eleven was obtained and the codes were not addressed by fewer than five participants. In contrast, looking at challenges in First Nations education, no more than nine participants indicated the same impediments in the interviews. In addition, there are categories solely referred to by three experts in education.

Evidently, challenges that were more elaborately discussed in the interviews presumably reveal their particular significance for the Australian educational context. Conversely, categories that were only addressed by a few participants might rather constitute individual experiences, yet this does not indicate a lower relevance. Thus, in addition to the bar chart in Figure 18, a matrix provides insights into the emphasis that participants attributed to different categories in the individual interviews:

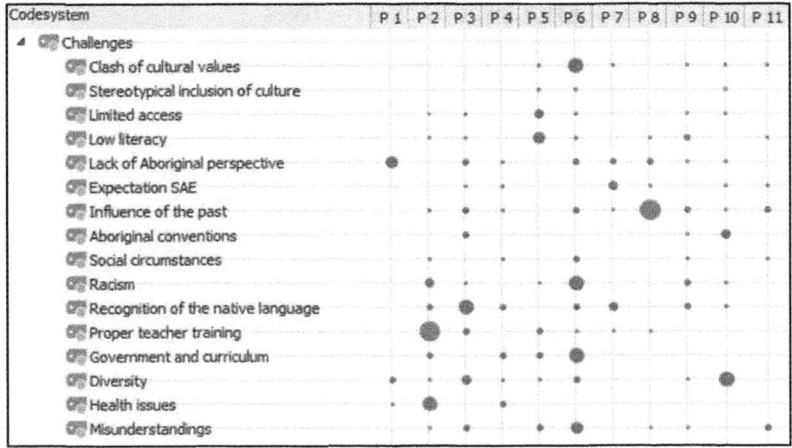

Figure 19: Code-Matrix-Browser: Challenges[40]

As demonstrated above, categories that played a particularly significant role for individual participants, indicated with a larger circle in Figure 19, include proper teacher training, clash of cultural values, racism, recognition of the home language, and influence of the past. The latter two codes are also positioned among the most commonly addressed challenges throughout all interviews. Looking at the obstacles identified by Indigenous participants, the categories that were strongly emphasized were the influence of the past, proper teacher training, health issues, and racism.

As with the influence of home language and culture, the frequency of the challenges addressed throughout the interviews may be indicative of their respective meaningfulness. Given the multitude of challenges in teaching and learning identified by the participants in the study, a call to action becomes apparent. Based on Figures 18 and 19, aspects relating to the recognition and diversity of Indigenous languages and cultures, the lack of Indigenous perspectives, proper teacher training as well as the likelihood of misunderstandings in Australian classrooms have been identified as core challenges in First Nations education. Most importantly, the influence of the past should not be underestimated but actively considered in teaching and learning contexts involving Indigenous students.

---

40   Image generated with MAXQDA12.

3.6 Incorporating Indigenous Perspectives

Building on the identified language- and culture-related factors as well as challenges in Australian First Nations education, this section provides insights into the significance attributed to incorporating Indigenous language and culture and recommends approaches and strategies to include Indigenous perspectives in teaching practice.

3.6.1 The Importance of Incorporating Indigenous Language and Culture

Aside from the open-ended questions in the explorative study, structurally identical rating questions on the importance of incorporating Indigenous Australian students' home language and culture for their learning were posed (see Appendix). Starting with a focus on Indigenous Australian learners' home language in school, interviewees were given a scale from one to ten, with one meaning *not important* and ten meaning *very important,* to evaluate the importance of including Indigenous Australian students' linguistic backgrounds in teaching materials and methodology for both English learning and general learning. Figure 20 outlines the participants' attributed importance:

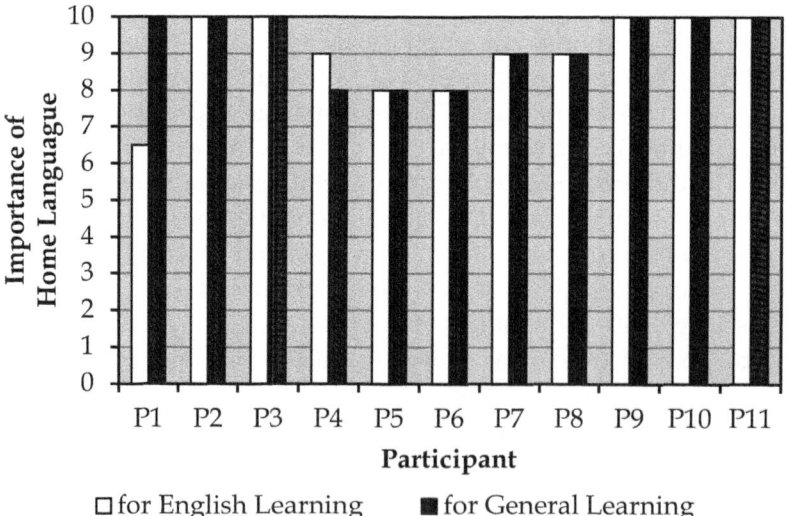

Figure 20: Importance of Incorporating Linguistic Backgrounds

Moving on to the importance of including Indigenous Australian learners' cultural backgrounds in classroom discourse, Figure 21 represents the data.

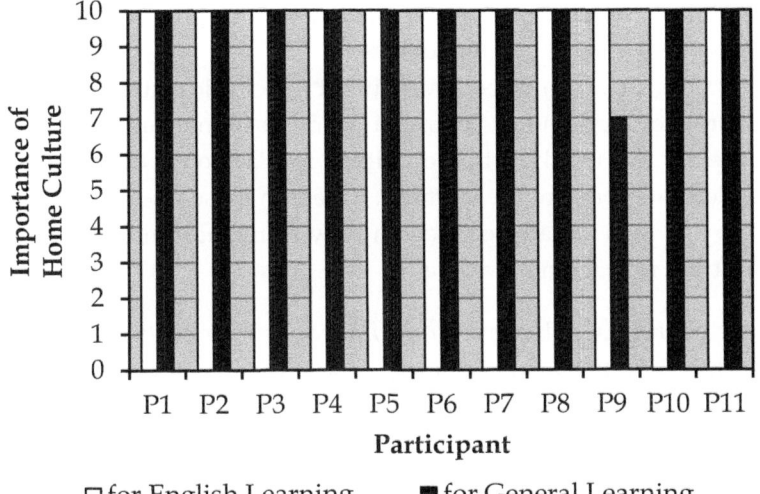

Figure 21: Importance of Incorporating Cultural Backgrounds

As can be seen in the two preceding figures, all participants regard the consideration and incorporation of Indigenous Australian students' home language and culture as important for learning. In particular, seven of the eleven experts rated the significance of the home language as a nine or a ten, thus as vital for both general and English learning in school.

Overall, a certain amount of non-homogeneity among the participants' assessments of the importance of incorporating students' home language for learning is noticeable. With the exception of P1, who greatly differentiates between the importance for English and general learning, almost no discrepancy is discernible among the remaining interviewees' evaluations as they rated students' home language as equally important both for English and general learning. On the contrary, taking Indigenous Australian students' home culture into account in teaching materials and methodology is almost uniformly seen as very important. Only P9 seems to hold a different view on the specific importance of the home culture for general learning and could thereby constitute an outlier in this evaluation. Hence, there are nuances to be observed between the two figures as culture is seen as very important while a slight unevenness in the participants' assessments regarding the significance of the home language can be perceived.

Overall, it can be concluded that the consideration and incorporation of Indigenous Australian students' home language and, to a greater extent, their home culture in classroom contexts is regarded as important for learning. Based on these findings, it is necessary to provide approaches on how to include Indigenous perspectives in teaching practice.

3.6.2 Strategies for Incorporating First Nations Perspectives

Having established the significance of incorporating Indigenous Australian students' linguistic and cultural backgrounds in educational contexts in the previous section, relevant suggestions and approaches will now be presented. As the participants in the study proposed various ideas for considering and including Indigenous perspectives in teaching materials and methodology, a different manner of presentation was chosen. Specifically, recommendations were grouped together depending on whether they related to teaching methodology, materials or staff. The following three lists thus constitute compilations of strategies to assist and encourage teachers to increasingly consider Indigenous Australian perspectives in teaching and learning. Moreover, the strategies might supply educators in multicultural classroom settings in and outside Australia with ideas and approaches for how to be increasingly mindful of their students' diverse backgrounds.

Teaching Methodology

In relation to teaching methodology, the participants emphasized the following approaches for the increasing inclusion of Indigenous perspectives in educational discourse:

- Inclusion of peer support activities and group work
- Using storytelling and yarning

- Involvement of family and community
- Adjustment of classroom language
- No expectation of proficiency in SAE and no overemphasis on mistakes in English
- Respect towards Indigenous Australian students' home languages by learning some expressions or phrases
- Maintenance of a good and strong relationship with students
- Application of culturally sensitive/responsive teaching approach
- Awareness of tendencies in Indigenous learning styles
- Using songs and stories to impart contents
- Inclusion of Indigenous students' worldview and interests
- Using students as teachers

Teaching Materials

Aside from teaching methodology, the participants also identified the following aspects as vital for making teaching materials more inclusive of Indigenous Australian perspectives:

- Using relevant and authentic materials
- Inclusion of Indigenous characters in materials
- Using texts and songs in the home language
- Using visuals and concrete material
- Using personalized learning
- Using comparative or bilingual resources
- Using materials specifically supporting literacy skills
- Consideration of culturally appropriate testing methods
- Organization of language and culture projects and programs
- Inclusion of songs, rhymes and stories
- Support of technological resources for languages and culture (apps, eBooks, etc.)

Teaching Staff

Finally, in addition to teaching materials and methodology, participants in the study also referred to teaching staff and identified four dimensions as relevant for Indigenous perspectives:

- Inclusion of Indigenous teachers or teaching assistants
- Involvement of Indigenous communities and families
- Support from specialist teachers or ESL teachers
- Exchange of effective materials and ideas with other educators

At this stage, the significance and actual impact of the suggested approaches and strategies on Indigenous Australian students' learning outcomes cannot be assessed. However, in order to exemplify how several of the aforementioned aspects can actively be included in teaching practice, Margaret James's textbook series the *Honey Ant Readers* is presented and analyzed in the upcoming sections.

3.6.3 Analysis of the Honey Ant Readers Textbooks

Created by Australian author and linguist Margaret James, the *Honey Ant Readers* (HARs) textbooks are specifically designed for Indigenous Australian learners, assisting them in their transition from AE to SAE by means of culturally relevant contents. As will be demonstrated in the course of this chapter, the HARs incorporate several dimensions identified by the experts in the interview study. The analysis provided in the following does not claim to be indicative of the textbooks' effectiveness, but attempts to reveal different ways of making Indigenous perspectives visible in teaching materials and methodology. After a brief introduction to the HARs, drawing on information obtained in an interview with the author (James 2015b), as well as the comprehensive *Honey Ant Readers teacher's book* (James 2015a), two textbooks are analyzed according to the criteria and results from the interview study.

Genesis and Objectives

Indigenous Australian learners' frequent disengagement and disinterest in reading and learning has been connected to an identified lack of appropriate print literature and reading materials. Authors predominantly focused on collecting stories told by Aboriginal learners, but there had not been any textbooks promoting the recognition of AE and Indigenous cultures. Thus, a community-based program to foster literacy skills was initiated at a school in Alice Springs based on the desire to support students by incorporating their home language and culture in classroom materials and methodology. Focus groups with teachers, parents, and community members, as well as surveys and recordings of learners' conversations and storytelling, allowed Margaret James to identify difficulties experienced by students in the transition from AE to SAE. In the HARs, this linguistic data is combined with theories from second language acquisition and is embedded in cultural contents and stories provided by local Elders (see Chapter III.3.2). Consequently, the HARs allow Indigenous students to "learn to read using their stories" (James 2014, 81) and thus constitute learning materials that are both "culturally and linguistically relevant to learners" (ibid., 82). Referring to the identified deficit view prevalent in learning contexts involving Indigenous learners (see Chapter IV.5), the author described the following overall aim of the HARs:

> I wanted to bring in their language and also, I wanted to turn around this thing that every Aboriginal kid going to school believed they would fail and I wanted to turn it around so they could believe that they would succeed and give them an experience of success. (James 2015b)

More specifically, the HARs consist of 20 books, in increasing stages of proficiency, in which a total of 650 expressions are "progressively introduced and repeated" (James 2014, 83) with the aim of establishing print literacy skills and building students' proficiency in SAE. Adhering to "natural stages of second language acquisition" (ibid., 79), the HARs gradually lead readers from a light version of AE, which James refers to as the "language of the playground" functioning as a lingua franca among Aboriginal learners, to SAE. Using a sequence from familiar forms to unfamiliar structures throughout the books, the acquisition of sounds is the main focus, though aspects of morphology and syntax are also of central importance (James 2015a, 1–4). Moreover, phonemes that can also be found in traditional languages are introduced first and illustrations take up a lot of space at the beginning, while the focus gradually shifts to less familiar phonemes and graphic support is reduced. As the author puts it, "[t]he objective of the HARs is to get children reading/decoding, since, once they can read, they will be able to transfer those decoding skills to SAE" (James 2015a, 9).

Analysis

For the purpose of providing a practical example of incorporating Indigenous Australian perspectives in teaching materials and methodology, two books from the twenty-part HAR textbook series are examined: book 7, *Stop Dog* (James 2013) and the more advanced book 14, *Big Man Grab Sister* (James 2010). In connection with the central categories identified in the study, the following criteria are used for the analysis and are discussed under the following headings using characteristic examples:

- Storytelling Methodology
- Culturally Relevant Contents
- Recognition of Aboriginal English
- Concept of Orality
- Learning through songs and rhymes

Storytelling Methodology

As meaning and morals are conveyed and information is imparted in an indirect manner using one story per book, traditional storytelling is evident in the HARs with *Nana*, the grandmother, functioning as the main character and storyteller. Moreover, the use of generic terms like *little sister* or *big man* constitutes another common feature of storytelling methodology, ensuring that all community members can relate to the characters in the story. James (2015a) clarifies that the stories were "[d]eveloped from the ground up, in collaboration with Aboriginal Elders, community members and children" (2015a, 4). While some of them are "based on real-life events, […] others are inspired by stories that Aboriginal Elders have shared with the author" (James 2015a, 2). Figure 22 demonstrates the storytelling methodology.

Figure 22: Storytelling Methodology in the HARs[41]

Constituting a culturally relevant Indigenous methodology, storytelling (see Chapter IV.2.2) ties in with the following aspect related to culturally relevant contents included in the HARs.

Culturally Relevant Contents

James asserts that the HARs "have been developed to suit the particular needs of Central Australian Indigenous children; their language, their dominant interests and their experience of life" (James 2010, 36). Both of the books analyzed are set in the Australian desert and depict Aboriginal students going to school or spending time

---

[41] Image retrieved from James 2010, 19.

with their family and their community. As the author puts it, the "themes, stories and figures in the Readers reflect Indigenous culture. Set in the red sandy desert of Central Australia, the stories are about traditional family life, including hunting and gathering" (James 2015a, 2). The following figure depicts the incorporation of culturally relevant contents in the HARs:

Figure 23: **Culturally Relevant Contents in the HARs**[42]

As can be seen in Figure 23, the stories depict the home environment and portray past and present experiences in the life of Indigenous learners in Central Australia, such as digging for honey ants or chasing a goanna. Moreover, cultural concepts such as the importance of community and relationships are expressed. Instead of proper names, roles within the community are used for the individual characters, e.g. *sister*, *kids*, *Nana*, etc. (James 2014).

Hence, the books promote Indigenous Australian perspectives and present stories which are "consistent with the learners' knowledge, culture and experience of the world" (James 2014, 82). Through the portrayal of Indigenous characters, the students are able to see themselves in the materials. Moreover, as they can relate to the stories, which mirror their interests and experiences, learner engagement can be promoted and (reading) motivation increased.

---

[42] Image retrieved from James 2013, 38–39.

Recognition of Aboriginal English

The author outlines that the "language of the HARs moves from the oral language the learners hear and speak in the playground, to colloquial SAE according to the natural order in which speakers of other languages have been shown to acquire the grammatical structures of Standard English" (2015a, 14). In fact, the HARs introduce new words, not according to their meaning, but according to their level of difficulty for Indigenous children. For instance, *school* might be an easy word for many English language learners but since traditional Indigenous languages do not usually comprise double consonant phonemes in their sound system, the correct pronunciation of such words can be challenging for Indigenous students (James 2013, 68–72). Titling book 14 *Big Man Grab Sister* rather than the SAE equivalent of ***The** Big Man **Grabs the** Sister*, the HARs consistently pay respect to AE and appreciate its worth and validity. Finally, the volumes only introduce a limited number of new expressions at a time, in order to uphold the students' confidence (James 2010, 36–40) Thus, as the books start out from light AE, vocabulary such as *fella, aunty* or *mob* are included in the HARs. Figure 24 illustrates the recognition of AE in the textbooks.

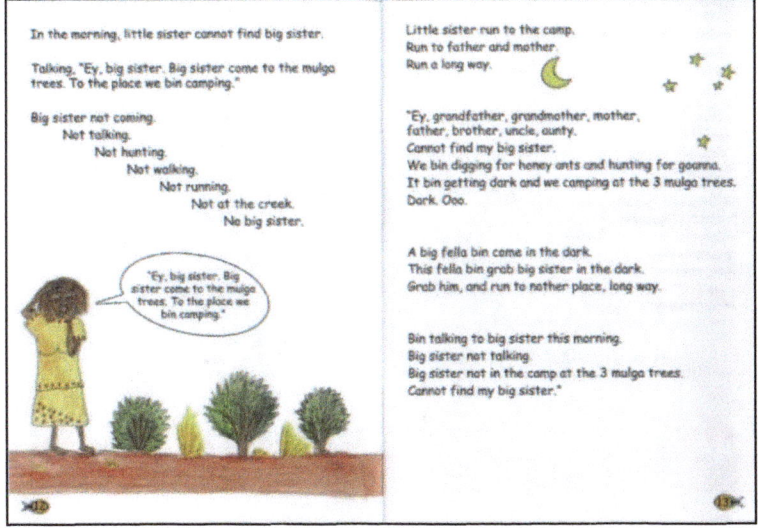

Figure 24: Recognition of AE in the HARs[43]

---

[43] Image retrieved from James 2010, 12–13.

Overall, the HARs follow a bidialectal approach as "AE (the dialect of identity) is valued and accommodated at the same time as the standard dialect (the dialect of power) is explicitly and systematically taught to facilitate learning in SAE" (James 2014, 82).

Concept of Orality

Building on the recognition of AE, the texts used in the HARs match the students' oral language use, i.e. students learn to read in the language they speak. In relation to the concept of orality of Indigenous languages and AE (see Chapter V.3.1.3), James observes that if "we read in a language that is similar to our spoken language, the only task is that of decoding the words, rather than searching for their meaning as well" (James 2015a, 8). Apart from the culturally relevant contents and the relation to the students' worldview facilitating the process of decoding letters and understanding words, the books also simulate spoken language use and include images and figures as tools to help students infer meaning.

Figure 25: Concept of Orality in the HARs[44]

---

[44] Image retrieved from James 2010, 6–7.

As can be seen in Figure 25, speech bubbles and pictures are used to facilitate students' understanding of the story. Moreover, as movement is imitated by the text, the formatting of *run, run, run* implies the meaning of the lexical item and thus supports the decoding process. Generally, the more advanced HAR book *Big Man Grab Sister* includes more text and a more complex story, whereas *Stop Dog* reveals little text per page and a foregrounding of pictures as an integral feature to ensure comprehension of the story. Among other learning styles evident in the HARs, the books include songs and rhymes, which James (2014, 83) describes as "powerful tools for Indigenous-language speaking learners who come from an oral background." The next section investigates this dimension further.

Learning through Songs and Rhymes

Examining the HARs, the implementation of several tendencies in Indigenous learning styles (see Chapter IV.2) can be observed. Specifically, grammar and pronunciation are frequently practiced through songs and rhymes, which constitutes a valuable approach for several reasons. On the one hand, when "singing, the learner imitates the rhythm, stress, pitch and patterns of a language, thereby becoming familiar with the pronunciation and syntax" (James 2013, 72). Moreover, "[g]roup singing is culturally appropriate for Aboriginal learners for whom 'shame' of being singled out is a significant inhibitor to language learning" (James 2014, 83) (see Chapter IV.2.3). Hence, songs and rhymes are "particularly comfortable ways to teach pronunciation and vocabulary" since in a "group situation there is no shame or embarrassment" (James 2015a, 22).

Thus, all HARs incorporate a number of songs with a specific language focus, helping to develop proficiency in oral SAE. As the materials were designed for speakers of traditional Indigenous languages or AE, James (2015a, 2) explains that

> [b]ased on research into the differences between these languages and English, the songs and rhymes address challenges that speakers of these languages are likely to face (for example, the pronunciation of 'v' or 'ch') or aspects of grammar, such as SAE past tense or question forms (for example, *'Have you been shopping?'* and *'Where did you live?'*).

Specifically, the songs in *Stop Dog* focus on practicing numbers and body parts whereas the elements of *Big Man Grab Sister* include difficult phonemes and further challenging aspects in SAE grammar, such as the third person "s." Figure 26 demonstrates the use of songs in the HARs and Figure 27 exemplifies the implementation of rhymes and their strong connection with the stories.

Figure 26: Songs in the HARs[45]

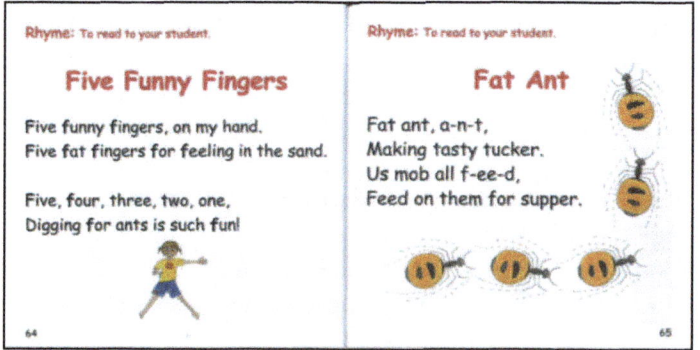

Figure 27: Rhymes in the HARs[46]

---

[45] Image retrieved from James 2010, 24–25.
[46] Image retrieved from James 2013, 64–65.

In the HARs teacher's book, James provides an abundance of additional resources and materials for teachers, including different games and activities, such as flash cards for vocabulary and conversation cards for developing storytelling skills in English (James 2015a).

Conclusion

In summary, the HARs constitute one of the few existing resources that educators in Australia can draw on to be inclusive of Indigenous Australian perspectives in their teaching practice. The analysis above demonstrates that the HARs implement several perspectives and approaches identified in the interview study as well as in the literature.

First, storytelling is used as an underlying methodology throughout the books, constituting a core element in Indigenous learning as highlighted in Yunkaporta's (2009) model (see Chapter IV.3.1). In addition, the HARs are mindful of other cultural tendencies in learning styles: concrete and contextualized ways of learning are employed by including the use of games, songs and rhymes. Moreover, the importance of recognizing students' home languages, with a particular focus on Aboriginal English, is expressed in the HARs, which acknowledge it as the basis of all understanding. By evidently supporting a two-way model and adopting a bidialectal approach (see Chapter IV.4.1.1), the HARs clearly aim at additive bilingualism and biliteracy. As such, the concept of orality is taken into consideration, as the HARs provide manifold tools to assist learners in decoding and meaning making. Apart from learning styles, the incorporation of Indigenous worldviews and Indigenous learners' lived experience and interest plays a vital role in the HARs. Through culturally relevant contents and the display of Indigenous characters, students receive opportunities for identification, which can effect a reinforcement of identity and pride.

Hence, the HARs actively integrate several of the language- and culture-related dimensions as well as suggested teaching approaches identified in the research study. Simultaneously, the HARs attend to certain of the challenges addressed in teaching and learning, such as the expectation of SAE, the recognition of home languages and lack of resources. Most importantly, the HARs provide a direct access to students' first languages, include Indigenous perspectives and thereby support students' literacy skills. Incontestably, the HARs constitute a valuable resource that exemplifies how classrooms can become more inclusive of Indigenous perspectives.

Apart from the amazing features of the books outlined above, there are also certain limitations, or possibilities for improvement, that should be addressed at this stage. To start with, in order to facilitate a more sophisticated two-way education model, non-Indigenous perspectives and non-Indigenous characters could be included in the HARs. Doing so would express a spirit of togetherness and connect linguistic and cultural heritage with present and future matters. Thus, Indigenous and non-Indigenous learners could function as both teachers and learners of their respective linguistic and cultural heritage, creating greater understanding and respect inside classrooms.

Apart from the many challenges to which the HARs attend, there still remains the non-negligible hurdle constituted by the great diversity of Aboriginal students and their languages as identified by the educators in the study. In the books, the focus lies predominantly on the environment and experiences of Indigenous students in Central Australia. As the everyday life and context of students living in QLD or NSW might look quite different, the materials either need to become more varied or else individual, context-specific versions of the HARs need to be produced.

In conclusion, the HARs incorporate several aspects of Indigenous Australian students' home language and culture that were identified as relevant in the study. Specifically, the HARs can be of valuable help in solving various challenges and, presumably, beneficially impact students' learning and engagement.

4. Summary and Discussion of Findings

As the results of the research project were presented in the preceding chapter, a synopsis of the major insights is provided in this section.

The findings are then combined with the literature in the field and discussed in relation to the study's underlying research questions.

4.1 Summary of Findings

The interview study revealed essential language- and culture-related factors as well as challenges for Indigenous Australian students' learning as illustrated in the generated coding schemes (see Figures 13, 14, and 17). Moreover, several strategies to incorporate Indigenous Australian perspectives in teaching practice were identified by the participants.

To start with, all of the education experts consulted regard the consideration and incorporation of Indigenous Australian students' home language and culture as important for their learning. In particular, being mindful of Indigenous students' cultural backgrounds in school was almost uniformly classified as very important. Despite the fact that a slight imbalance among the participants' evaluations was detected with regard to the significance of students' linguistic heritage, seven of the eleven interviewees still rated the importance of considering Indigenous Australian learners' home languages in teaching practice as a nine or a ten, i.e. very important. Also, there was very little discrepancy between the importance of students' backgrounds for their English or general learning in school.

The aspects most frequently highlighted in the interview study in connection with language-related factors essential for Indigenous Australian students' learning include the oral tradition of Indigenous languages, the recognition of students' home languages as well as the fact that students' linguistic background forms the basis of their understanding. Even though the importance of code-switching was only addressed by approximately half of the interviewees, two participants in particular elaborated on this aspect. Moreover, Indigenous students' home languages and cultures were designated as vital sources of pride and confidence for Indigenous learners by the education experts.

Referring to culture-related dimensions, the majority of participants in the study emphasized the importance of maintaining strong relationships and the acknowledgment of home values and attitudes towards learning. In this regard, most interviewees suggested the need for educators to take differing cultural concepts and culture-specific tendencies in learning styles into consideration in order to support all students as best as possible. Finally, other decisive factors concerned Indigenous Australian learners' worldviews and the significance of integrating families and communities in the learning processes.

Major existing challenges in teaching and learning with Indigenous Australian students identified by the experts in the study relate to the influence of the past, which received the highest number of references in the interviews, the great diversity among Indigenous learners as well as the lack of appropriate resources and teaching materials that are inclusive of Indigenous perspectives. An additional obstacle for Indigenous students in the Australian school setting, emerging from the data, constitutes shortcomings in teacher education in regards to Indigenous Australian ways of knowing, being, and doing; and, consequently, misunderstandings in classrooms, which over half of the participants identified. Specifically, the study re-emphasized the imperative for teachers to recognize Indigenous home languages (including traditional languages and AE) and understand that the majority of Indigenous students are ESL learners of English and thus require extra literacy support. Finally, Indigenous participants argued that aspects relating to health issues and racism can also significantly impede Indigenous students' learning.

Incorporating Indigenous perspectives in classroom discourse, making use of storytelling, building strong relationships, including songs and rhymes, integrating families and communities in learning processes, and incorporating Indigenous characters and worldviews in resources—these were all proposed in addition to further suggestions for teaching materials and methodology. The analysis of the *Honey Ant Readers* (James 2015a) demonstrates that the contents and rationale of the books tie in with various aspects that the experts in the study identified as decisive for Indigenous Australian students' learning. As discussed, the HARs incorporate traditional perspectives since their stories are based on Indigenous learners' worldviews and experiences and consider Indigenous pedagogies such as storytelling or learning through songs and rhymes. Furthermore, the reading materials acknowledge the oral tradition of students' home languages and especially show appreciation for Aboriginal English, which is actively included in the books.

4.2 Discussion of Findings

Having summarized the major outcomes of the research study, the findings can now be connected to the four research questions and contrasted with the existing literature in the field. The first core question to be discussed reads as follows:

RQ1: Which language-related factors do experienced educators perceive to impact Indigenous Australian students' learning in school?

The most salient dimension that this explorative study uncovered regarding RQ1 is the utmost importance of the recognition of Indigenous Australian learners' home languages as well as an awareness of the underlying concept of orality of Indigenous languages. As they traditionally were and continue to be spoken rather than written, and have predominantly been transmitted orally, students require extra support in school for building their general literacy skills. Thus, the significantly lower competences in reading and writing among Indigenous students in contrast to non-Indigenous learners might, among other aspects, be attributed to the oral tradition of Indigenous languages. Moreover, and strongly tied to the oral tradition, the importance of the recognition of Aboriginal English and the general acknowledgment of students' home languages were deemed essential. The study emphasizes that teachers need to acknowledge that English constitutes a second language or dialect for the majority of Indigenous students (see Chapter III.3.1). In this bidialectal-bilingual context, the development of code-switching abilities, i.e. being able to consciously shift from one language variety to another, was identified as essential for Indigenous students' learning.

In terms of connections between the language-related factors identified in the study and the related literature in the field, Malcolm (2018), James (2015a), and Eades (2014, 2013) also advocate for a greater recognition and consideration of Aboriginal English as a distinct variety of SAE in different contexts. Moreover, Malcolm and Truscott (2012) accentuate the importance of fostering AE, generally embracing Indigenous Australia's linguistic heritage, and promoting code-switching abilities in their two-way bidialectal model (see Chapter IV.4.1.1). In this regard, the empirical study on quality classroom practices for Indigenous learners by Lewthwaite et al. (2017) also highlights the development of code-switching abilities and the recognition of Indigenous students as second language learners of English as essential. Principally, the interviewed Indigenous learners in Lewthwaite et al.'s (2017) study endorsed educators that showed an understanding and appreciation of their linguistic heritage, which links with the findings from this study. Furthermore, the concept of orality of Indigenous languages, which all of the participants in the study addressed, was discussed by Windle (2009), was strongly integrated into the HARs (James 2015a), and features in the form of storytelling in Yunkaporta's (2009) eight ways of Aboriginal learning (see Chapter IV.3.1). Lastly, language constitutes a foundation for learning in Lowe et al.'s (2020) framework of culturally nourishing pedagogy. Specifically, acknowledging the significance of including Indigenous linguistic heritage forms part of their pillar of "cultural inclusion" (see Chapter IV.3.2).

Hence, the principal outcomes of the study concerning essential language-related factors for Indigenous Australian students' learning in school are compatible with the existing literature in the field.

The next core area of the research project investigated factors concerning students' cultural backgrounds meaningful for their learning in school based on the following question:

RQ2: *Which culture-related factors do experienced educators perceive to impact Indigenous Australian students' learning in school?*

Both the consideration of home values and attitudes towards education as well as community and family involvement in school were highlighted as vital factors for learning. Establishing and maintaining trustworthy and strong relationships between teachers and learners and among classmates was identified as an additional priority for Indigenous Australian students' learning. More precisely, the importance of home values, relationships, and tendencies in learning styles were not only among the most frequently addressed dimensions but were particularly emphasized by the Indigenous participants in the study. Connecting language and culture, a further decisive factor that emerged from the study relates to cultural concepts inherent in languages, which frequently render direct translations between Indigenous languages or AE and SAE impossible, such as vocabulary for numbers or seasons (see section 3.1.5). Generally, the findings emphasize the importance of building awareness of differing worldviews, values, and conventions inside the classroom and among students as constitutive for mutual understanding and successful learning in school. Finally, the research study demonstrates that both home language and culture can form a vital source of pride for Indigenous Australian students.

Several of the culture-related factors identified as essential for Indigenous Australian students' learning show clear links to previous discussions in the field of First Nations education. On the one hand, building strong relationships in educational settings involving Indigenous learners constitutes a core commitment at Worawa Aboriginal College (Hamilton 2015) as well as in schools employing a two-way bidialectal model (Malcolm & Truscott 2012). Moreover, the three approaches of *culturally nourishing pedagogy* (Lowe et al. 2020), *culturally responsive pedagogy* (Morisson et al. 2019) as well as the *Stronger Smarter Approach* (Sarra et al. 2018; Stronger Smarter Institute 2017) incorporate learning through relationships as central elements of their frameworks. On the other hand, research projects in the field have also identified relationship building as a key quality teaching practice in Indigenous education (Lewthwaite et al. 2017; Philips & Luke 2017; Donovan 2015; Milgate & Giles-Browne 2013).

In addition, the importance of involving community and family in school settings is also supported by other authors in the field (Lowe et al. 2020; Burgess et al. 2019; Stronger Smarter Institute 2017) and constitutes a distinct dimension in Yunkaporta's (2009) model. Moreover, scholars have discussed culture-specific tendencies in learning styles and advocated for concrete, collaborative and hands-on approaches (Harrison & Sellwood 2016; Malcolm & Truscott 2012; Yunkaporta 2009; Hughes et al. 2004).

Consequently, several culture-related outcomes of this research project are in alignment with aspects addressed in previous studies and discussions. Based on the language- and culture-related factors identified in this study, however, certain dimensions which have not yet been attended to extensively in the field emerge. While nuances might be deducible from Lowe et al.'s (2020) model as well as Lewthwaite et al.'s (2017) interview study of Indigenous views on quality teaching practice, the relevance of home values and attitudes towards education for student learning needs to be investigated more extensively. In addition, as potential causes for misunderstandings and impediments to learning, cultural concepts embedded in students' home languages need to constitute core objectives in future studies. Lastly, as evidence from the study suggests that home language and culture can constitute valuable sources of pride for Indigenous Australian learners in school, but also instill feelings of embarrassment, this ambivalence needs to be explored further.

In summary, in relation to essential language- and culture-related dimensions highlighted in the study, certain schools in Australia already implement ambitious approaches inclusive of Indigenous perspectives and approaches. However, authors such as Lowe et al. (2021) have advocated for an implementation of language and cultural programs in mainstream schooling on a larger scale, as they were able to reveal positive effects on Indigenous learners' identity, cultural knowledge and community connection. Thus, Lowe et al. (2021) emphasize the imperative for every school to "establish authentic and accessible local place-based programmes that affirm and strengthen students' cultural identities and their academic efficacy" (ibid., 89) and to "centre macro-issues of policy, funding and systemic structures to better support schools and communities in implementing language and culture programmes" (ibid., 91).

The third research question underpinning the study was concerned with existing challenges in First Nations education.

RQ3: Which challenges exist in teaching and learning with Indigenous Australian students according to experienced educators?

The challenges identified in the study range from the historical burden, the lack of Indigenous perspectives in teaching materials, and educators' lack of awareness and recognition of students' linguistic backgrounds, to impediments related to racism, health, and systemic shortcomings. Moreover, the great diversity of Indigenous languages and cultures as well as the limited access to relevant resources constitute another challenge that is unique to a multicultural classroom involving Indigenous Australian learners. Further obstacles derived from the interview data include misunderstandings, low literacy rates, and social circumstances. While these dimensions reveal various concerns in First Nations education, they also highlight areas that demand improvement in contemporary teacher training, which the Indigenous participants particularly emphasized in the research study.

Several of the challenges that surfaced in this research project have also been identified by other authors in the field. For instance, recent studies have explored the causes of lower literacy and achievement rates among Indigenous students (Lin et al. 2021; Guenther & Osborne 2020; Baxter & Meyers 2019). Authors have also extensively discussed the lack of teachers' knowledge and readiness to recognize and include Indigenous perspectives in their practice, and criticized the prevailing deficit views and negative conceptions in education (Burgess et al. 2019; Moodie et al. 2019; Vass et al. 2019; Malcolm 2018; Sarra et al. 2018; Philips & Luke 2017; Lloyd et al. 2015). Moreover, various authors (Sarra et al. 2018; Lewthwaite et al. 2017; Power et al. 2015) address the influence of the past, which was identified as a relevant factor potentially impeding Indigenous students' learning in the study. Major concerns in the recent literature also refer to racism (Daniels-Mayes 2020; Moodie et al. 2019) as well as systemic shortcomings in the Australian school system and its related policies (Lowe et al. 2020; Morisson et al. 2019). In addition, Donovan (2015) criticizes the frequent lack of Indigenous perspectives inside classrooms while Partington and Galloway (2007) refer to health and socio-economic impediments to learning. Finally, Eades (2013) addresses challenges in connection with differing cultural practices and customs, including the ever-present possibility of their causing misunderstandings in school.

In conclusion, while some of the identified challenges have been addressed by a large number of authors and supported by empirical data, the three principal challenges identified in the study—the influence of the past, the great diversity among Indigenous learners and the lack of Indigenous perspectives in teaching materials—have not been sufficiently investigated yet. Thorpe et al. (2021, 70) thus highlight the "importance of Aboriginal voice in acknowledging and understanding the impact of colonisation and ongoing injustices, and the criticality of bringing this knowledge into the curriculum" (Thorpe et al. 2021, 70). Moreover, the challenges identified highlight the imperative to provide improved teacher education to render classroom practice increasingly inclusive of First Nations perspectives. While this has been advocated by numerous scholars in the field (e.g. Donovan 2015), Thorpe et al. (2021) have recently provided evidence for the positive effects of place-based training courses led by Aboriginal communities on pre-service teachers' knowledge and awareness, as well as the development of a critical consciousness towards their own teaching practice.

Finally, the fourth research question reads as follows:

RQ4: *How can Indigenous Australian students' home language and culture be incorporated in teaching materials and methodology according to experienced educators?*

The diverse strategies proposed in the research study were concerned with teaching methodology, materials and staff. Related to some of the factors identified in RQ1 and RQ2, approaches suggested for incorporating Indigenous language and culture in teaching methodology include the formation of strong relationships with students, employing peer support and collaborative activities, involving the community, using storytelling and songs, and appreciating learners' linguistic heritage.

Moreover, teaching materials need to depict Indigenous characters, include relevant contents and support learning through visuals. In this regard, the inclusion of comparative bilingual resources or authentic learning materials in the students' first languages to provide access to their linguistic heritage are beneficial. Lastly, in connection with teaching staff, the study reveals the importance of collaborating with Indigenous teachers and teaching assistants and the involvement of communities and families in learning processes.

As can be seen, many of these proposed strategies constitute elements of the presented frameworks for First Nations education (see Chapter IV.3) and form part of the approaches adopted in specific Australian schools (see Chapter IV.4). In addition, Indigenous Australian learners', parents' and teachers' views on effective teaching practice constitute a recent research dimension in First Nations education. While authors have repeatedly emphasized the importance of building strong and trustworthy relationships with students and communities and showing an appreciation of learners' linguistic and cultural backgrounds (Guenther, Harrison & Burgess 2019; Philips & Luke 2017; Lewthwaite et al. 2017; Donovan 2015; Milgate & Giles-Browne 2013), they seem rather to dwell on outlining contemporary shortcomings, rarely providing actual recommendations for teaching practice. Thus, the strategies proposed in this study might serve as valuable starting points for educators in multicultural classrooms with a particular focus on Indigenous Australian learners.

5. Implications for Teaching Practice

On the basis of the findings of the qualitative research study, as well as the literature review in the field of First Nations education in Australia, several implications for educators working in multicultural classrooms can be deduced. The purpose of this section is to provide the impetus for a teaching practice in linguistically and culturally diverse learning settings that derives from the insights gained in the Indigenous Australian context.

Raising Awareness

Fundamentally, educators need to create an awareness of the existing multitude of factors connected to students' home language and culture. These are mostly tacit but can impact learning in various ways. Moreover, teachers need to realize that refusing to maintain a sensitive attitude towards learners' linguistic and cultural backgrounds may lead to misunderstandings, embarrassment, and a poor teacher-student relationship, which would likely result in students' disengagement from learning. Therefore, learners' diverse backgrounds need to be attended to with respect and diligence in school and teachers need to be mindful of the various dimensions that can be significant for learning as highlighted in the research study.

Acknowledging Students as Second Language/Dialect Speakers

The fact that the home language of an increasing number of students around the world is not the predominant language of instruction has to be taken into greater consideration by educators. This reality means that students are required to learn a new, i.e. second, language or dialect while receiving input in that very language. The ensuing consequences for learning need to be considered and potential disadvantages ought to be anticipated in school in order to secure a supportive learning environment. For instance, as advocated in the study, teachers engaged in First Nations education need to acknowledge that the majority of Indigenous Australian students are second language learners of English as they may speak a traditional Indigenous language or AE at home. Thus, due to the concept of orality, as well as to differences in the cultural concepts embedded in language, Indigenous Australian students might require extra literacy support as they might not have achieved literacy in their home language before entering formal education.

Hence, teachers should not generally expect high proficiency levels of English as doing so can cause frustration and have detrimental effects on student motivation and engagement.

Connecting to Students' Identities and Backgrounds

Teachers in multicultural classrooms need to educate themselves on the peculiarities of their students' cultural backgrounds, as the culture-specific conventions and values attributed to education are of particular significance for learning processes. Specifically, educators need to be mindful of the fact that students and their families might hold differing expectations of school, value education differently and reveal divergent preferences regarding learning. These factors can impact students' behavior and engagement with learning in class. In order to learn about students' diverse identities and backgrounds, questions such as the following can provide starting points for conversations or yarning circles using storytelling methodology:

- What is the value of learning and education for my students?
- What is the value of learning and education for my students' family and community?
- What are my students' expectations of school, the teachers, and the other learners?
- What are my students' parents' expectations of school, the teachers, and the other learners?
- How do my students prefer to learn?
- What are impediments to my students' successful learning?

In order to find out about these aspects, reaching out and getting support from community or family members and including them in teaching and learning processes are strategies suggested in the research study and supported in the literature review. Finally, educators should learn some expressions in students' home languages to show respect and openly express appreciation of the value and validity of their linguistic backgrounds. This may in turn encourage students' motivation and learning engagement, as they feel acknowledged and valued.

Building Strong Relationships

One salient aspect that emerges both from the research study as well as the literature review is the need to build strong and trustworthy relationships with learners and to hold high expectations of them. Hence, aside from connecting with families and communities, learners themselves need to be acknowledged as experts in their linguistic and cultural heritage and carefully included as valuable resources in classroom discourse. Thus, letting students act as teachers supports the emergence of a respectful learning environment based on mutual understanding and appreciation of students' cultural backgrounds and identity since everybody is learning together. Due to the ambivalence identified between pride and embarrassment, however, it is vital that culture is not included in a tokenistic, superficial manner, which fosters stereotyping and essentializing, but that its complex and diverse nature is expressed and its importance and omnipresence is acknowledged.

Openness towards a Variety of Perspectives

Generally, educators ought to frame their teaching practice openly in order to allow and acknowledge the existence of multiple perspectives in the classroom. Thus, including students' different worldviews, experiences, and opinions about a subject area, thereby adopting multiple vantage points, is an essential method for multicultural classrooms in a global age. Through this openness towards a variety of viewpoints and by appreciation of the diversity of learners and their backgrounds inside one classroom, an important step away from the prevailing deficit views is taken.

In conclusion, particularly in the light of the increasing scope of cultural diversity in global classrooms, authors have advocated for adopting a strength-based approach, in which relationships and mutual respect are central. Specifically, "[f]ocusing on the strengths that students bring to the classroom encourages a strong sense of cultural identity and sense of belonging in a supportive, high-expectations student learning environment" (Sarra et al. 2018, 34). As learners (and teachers) are all different in different ways, students can learn from and with each other by means of the Indigenous pedagogy of *storytelling* and thereby work together in a respectful and supportive environment, one which needs to be established in all schools. By this means, a big step towards inclusive educational practices would be achieved.

Chapter VI

Conclusion and Outlook

This book has presented findings from a qualitative research study conducted in Australia, a country acclaimed for its linguistic and cultural diversity. Specifically, the educational context of Indigenous Australian learners was investigated by shedding light on the incorporation of First Nations perspectives in teaching materials and methodology as well as by identifying language- and culture-related factors in and challenges to successful learning in contemporary education. Through semi-guided interviews with eleven experts in First Nations education, including both Indigenous and non-Indigenous teachers, principals, university professors, and teaching assistants, a variety of perspectives was captured. Fundamentally, the explorative research study confirmed the presumption that a consideration and incorporation of Indigenous Australian students' home language and culture in school is vital for their learning. By drawing on participants' wealth of experience, a multiplicity of language- as well as culture-related factors underpinning effective schooling for Indigenous Australian students was raised to the surface and generated insightful coding schemes. Moreover, the study revealed several challenges in Indigenous education, highlighted certain complexities arising in connection with the incorporation of First Nations perspectives in classroom discourse, and pointed to necessary dimensions for improvement that are in alignment with the recent literature in the field. Finally, several strategies and recommendations for teaching practice in multicultural classroom settings were proposed in the study.

Looking at future research directions, the findings from the qualitative study can form the basis for quantitative and longitudinal investigations of concrete cause-and-effect correlations between the individual dimensions and Indigenous Australian students' learning outcomes. Based on the frequency of the identified factors, suppositions regarding their respective significance for student learning can be inferred, yielding hypotheses like the following: *Indigenous Australian students' learning outcomes will be positively influenced if teaching materials include Indigenous characters, perspectives and worldviews.*

Moreover, quantitative, large-scale studies are required to identify approaches that are already adopted in schools and examine which dimensions need to be the focus of future directions in teacher education. Lastly, as multicultural classrooms are not only found in Australia but are an increasing reality in educational institutions around the world, the generated coding schemes could be contrasted with categories obtained in other linguistically and culturally diverse contexts by means of similar, qualitative studies. Thus, the interview study conducted necessary preparatory work for such ensuing quantitative and longitudinal or comparative qualitative studies.

In summary, the findings emphasize the need for educators' increased awareness of and sensitivity to learners' diverse backgrounds as contributing factors to effective learning. As shown in the study, building strong relationships with students, connecting with community and family, and learning from each other in an environment characterized by openness, mutual respect, and readiness to engage constitute the key elements of a fruitful multicultural classroom pedagogy. In order to overcome the multiplicity of contemporary impediments to successful learning in Australian First Nations education, there is an urgent need for improved teacher education as expressed in the research findings. In order to facilitate learning and potentially also collaboration in other fields, an approximation between Indigenous and non-Indigenous ways of knowing, being, and doing through knowledge and awareness building has to be foregrounded, as illustrated in Yunkaporta's (2009) boomerang matrix (Figure 8). Specifically, educators need to recognize and become increasingly aware of their students' linguistic and cultural backgrounds in order to foster the learning processes for all students in class. As current research trends in First Nations education have been shown to attend to the dimension of enhanced teacher education, there is hope for an improved future in which all students are supported as best as possible.

Therefore, at the end of this book, I would like to refer back to the introductory chapter in which Nelson Mandela eloquently stated:

Education is the most powerful weapon which you can use to change the world.

At the end of this research project, I would like to add a perspective to these meaningful words and conclude:

Education can only be successful if students are met where they are, linguistically and culturally.

Bibliography

Arthur, J.M. 1996. *Aboriginal English: a cultural study*. Melbourne: Oxford University Press.

Australian Bureau of Statistics. 2017a. "Cultural Diversity in Australia". Released 28 June 2017. Census of Population and Housing: Reflecting Australia—Stories from the Census, 2016. https://www.abs.gov.au/ausstats/abs@.nsf/Lookup/by%20Subject/2016~Main%20Features~Cultural%20Diversity%20Article~60.

Australian Bureau of Statistics. 2017b. "Aboriginal and Torres Strait Islander Population". Released 28 June 2017. Census of Population and Housing: Reflecting Australia—Stories from the Census, 2016. https://www.abs.gov.au/ausstats/abs@.nsf/Lookup/by%20Subject/2071.0~2016~Main%20Features~Aboriginal%20and%20Torres%20Strait%20islander%20Population%20Article~12#.

Australian Bureau of Statistics. 2018. "Estimates of Aboriginal and Torres Strait Islander Australians". Released 31 August 2018. https://www.abs.gov.au/statistics/people/aboriginal-and-torres-strait-islander-peoples/estimates-aboriginal-and-torres-strait-islander-australians/jun-2016.

Australian Bureau of Statistics. 2021. "Schools: Aboriginal and Torres Strait Islander students". Released 19 February 2021. https://www.abs.gov.au/statistics/people/education/schools/2020#aboriginal-and-torres-strait-islander-students.

Australian Curriculum, Assessment and Reporting Authority (ACARA). 2015. National Assessment Program—Literacy and Numeracy Achievement in Reading, Writing, Language Conventions and Numeracy: National Report for 2015

Australian Curriculum, Assessment and Reporting Authority (ACARA). 2019. *National Assessment Program—Literacy and Numeracy Achievement in Reading, Writing, Language Conventions and Numeracy: National Report for 2019*

Australian Curriculum, Assessment and Reporting Authority (ACARA). n.d.a. "Intercultural Understanding". Accessed 30 April 2021. https://australiancurriculum.edu.au/f-10-curriculum/general-capabilities/intercultural-understanding/.

Australian Curriculum, Assessment and Reporting Authority (ACARA). n.d.b. "Aboriginal and Torres Strait Islander Histories and Cultures". Accessed 30 April 2021. https://www.australiancurriculum.edu.au/f-10-curriculum/cross-curriculum-priorities/aboriginal-and-torres-strait-islander-histories-and-cultures/.

Baker, C. 2011. *Foundations of bilingual education and bilingualism.* 5th edn. Clevedon, England: Multilingual Matters.

Baker, W. 2015. *Culture and identity through English as a Lingua Franca. Rethinking concepts and goals in intercultural communication.* Berlin/Boston: De Gruyter Mouton.

Baker, C., and Wright, W. E. 2017. *Foundations of Bilingual Education and Bilingualism.* 6th edn. Bristol: Multilingual Matters.

Ball, J. and Bernhardt, B.M.H. 2012. "Standard English as a second dialect: a Canadian perspective." In *Rethinking education volume 5: harnessing linguistic variation to improve education,* edited by A. Yiakoumetti, 189–226. Bern: Peter Lang.

Baxter, L.P., and Meyers, N.M. 2019. "What counts? The influence of school attendance on Australia's urban Indigenous students' educational achievement." *The Australian Educational Researcher* 46: 511–532. https://doi.org/10.1007/s13384-019-00300-y.

Bierwirth, A., Blell, G., and Fuchs, S. 2017. „Wie divers ist Englischlernen? Konzepte in Forschung und Praxis zum inklusiven Englischunterricht." *Zeitschrift Für Inklusion* 3: chapter 3. https://www.inklusion-online.net/index.php/inklusion-online/article/view/447.

Board of Studies NSW. 2010. "Timeline 1967–2007". Last updated 21 January 2010. http://ab-ed.boardofstudies.nsw.edu.au/go/aboriginal-studies/timeline/timeline-1967-2007.

Boon, H.J. and Lewthwaite, B.E. 2016. "Signatures of quality teaching for Indigenous students." *Australian Journal of Teacher Education* 43: 453–471. https://doi.org/10.1007/s13384-016-0209-4.

Brinkmann, S., and Kvale, S. 2015. *InterViews: learning the craft of qualitative research interviewing.* 3rd edn. Thousand Oaks, CA: SAGE.

Brown, H.D. 2007, *Teaching by principles: an interactive approach to language pedagogy.* 3rd edn. New York, NY: Pearson.

Burgess, C., Tennent, C. Vass, G., Guenther, J., Lowe, K., and Moodie, N. 2019. "A systematic review of pedagogies that support, engage and improve the educational outcomes of Aboriginal Students." *The Australian Educational Researcher* 46, no. 2: 297–318. https://doi.org/10.1007/s13384-019-00315-5.

Carter, R., and Nunan, D. 2001. "Introduction." In *The Cambridge guide to teaching English to speakers of other languages,* edited by R. Carter and D. Nunan, 1–6. Cambridge: Cambridge University Press.

Churchill, S. 1986. *The education of linguistic and cultural minorities in the OECD countries.* Clevedon, England: Multilingual Matters.

Closing the Gap in Partnership. 2020. "National Agreement on Closing the Gap". https://www.closingthegap.gov.au/.

Council of Europe. 2001. *Common European Framework of Reference for Languages: Learning, teaching, assessment*. Strasbourg: Cambridge University Press.

Daniels-Mayes, S. 2020. "A courageous conversation with racism: revealing the racialised stories of Aboriginal deficit for pre-service teachers". *The Australian Educational Researcher* 47: 537–554. https://doi.org/10.1007/s13384-019-00360-0.

Dockery, A.M. 2010. "Culture and wellbeing: the case of Indigenous Australians". *Social Indicators Research* 99, no. 2: 315–332.

Donovan, M.J. 2015. "Aboriginal student stories, the missing voice to guide us towards change." *The Australian Educational Researcher* 42: 613–625.

Dooley, K. 2009. "Language and inclusion in mainstream classrooms." In *Culturally and linguistically diverse classrooms: new dilemmas for teachers*, edited by J. Miller, A. Kostogriz, and M. Gearon, 75–91. Bristol: Multilingual Matters.

Dresing, T. and Pehl, T. 2015. *Praxisbuch Interview, Transkription & Analyse: Anleitungen und Regelsysteme für qualitative Forschende*. 6th edn. Marburg: self-published.

Eagleson, R. D., Kaldor, S., and Malcolm, I.G. 1982. *English and the Aboriginal Child*. Canberra: Curriculum Development Centre.

Eades, D. 2013. *Aboriginal ways of using English*. Canberra, ACT: Aboriginal Studies Press.

Eades, D. 2014. "Aboriginal English." In *The Languages and Linguistics of Australia* edited by H. Koch and R. Nordlinger, 417–447. Berlin/Boston: De Gruyter Mouton.

Edmondson, W. J. and House, J. 2011. *Einführung in die Sprachlehrforschung*. 4th edn. Tübingen: Francke.

Education Council 2017. "National Aboriginal and Torres Strait Islander Education Strategy 2015". Last modified 17 November 2017. https://www.dese.gov.au/indigenous-education/resources/national-aboriginal-and-torres-strait-islander-education-strategy-2015.

Ellis, E., Gogolin, I., and Clyne, M. 2010. "The Janus face of monolingualism: a comparison of German and Australian language education policies". *Current Issues in Language Planning* 11, no. 4: 439–460.

Fäcke, C., and Meißner, F.-J. 2019. „Einleitung." In *Handbuch Mehrsprachigkeits- und Mehrkulturalitätsdidaktik* edited by C. Fäcke and F.-J. Meißner, 1–16. Tübingen: Narr.

García, O. 2009. *Bilingual education in the 21st century: a global perspective*. Electronic book. Chichester, UK: Wiley-Blackwell.

García, O., Flores, N., and Woodley, H. H. 2012. "Transgressing monolingualism and bilingual dualities: translanguaging pedagogies." In *Rethinking education volume 5: harnessing linguistic variation to improve education,* edited by A. Yiakoumetti, 45–76. Bern: Peter Lang.

Gearon, M. 2009. "Educating languages teachers for multilingual and multicultural settings". In *Culturally and linguistically diverse classrooms: new dilemmas for teachers,* edited by J. Miller, A. Kostogriz, and M. Gearon, 196–212. Bristol: Multilingual Matters.

Guenther, J., Harrison, N. and Burgess, C. 2019. "Special issue. Aboriginal voices: Systematic reviews of indigenous education." *The Australian Educational Researcher* 46, no. 2: 207–211. https://doi.org/10.1007/s13384-019-00316-4.

Guenther, J. and Osborne 2020. "Did DI do it? The impact of a programme designed to improve literacy for Aboriginal and Torres Strait Islander students in remote schools." *Australian Journal of Indigenous Education* 163–170. https://doi.org/10.1017/jie.2019.28.

Hamilton, M. 2015. *Walking together to make a difference: a case study of Worawa Aboriginal College.* http://www.worawa.vic.edu.au/walking-together-to-make-a-difference/.

Harkins, J. 1994. *Bridging two worlds: Aboriginal English and crosscultural understanding.* St Lucia, Queensland: University of Queensland Press. Foreword by D. Eades.

Harris, S. 1990. *Two-way Aboriginal schooling: education and cultural survival.* Canberra, ACT: Aboriginal Studies Press.

Harris, J. 2007. "Linguistic responses to contact: pidgins and creoles." In *Trends in linguistics: the habitat of Australia's Aboriginal languages: past, present, future,* edited by G. Leitner and I.G. Malcolm, 131–152. Berlin: Walter de Gruyter.

Harrison, N., Tennent, C., Vass, G., Guenther, J., Lowe, K., and Moodie, N. 2019. "Curriculum and learning in Aboriginal and Torres Strait Islander education: A systematic review." *The Australian Educational Researcher* 46, no. 2: 233–251. https://doi.org/10.1007/s13384-019-00311-9.

Hofstede, G. and McCrae R.R. 2004. "Personality and culture revisited: linking traits and dimensions of culture." *Cross-Cultural Research* 38, no. 1: 52–88.

Hollins, E. R. 2015, *Culture in school learning: revealing the deep meaning,* 3rd edn, Routledge, New York.

Hornberger, N. 2009. "Multilingual Education Policy and Practice: Ten Certainties (Grounded in Indigenous Experience)." In *Language Teaching* 42, no. 2: 197–211. http://dx.doi.org/10.1017/S0261444808005491.

Hughes, P., More, A. J., and Williams, M. 2004. *Aboriginal ways of learning.* Adelaide: Flinders Press.

James, M. 2010. *Big Man Grab Sister.* Alice Springs: Honey Ant Readers.

James, M. 2013. *Stop Dog: teacher's edition.* 3rd edn. Alice Springs: Honey Ant Readers.

James, M. 2014. "The Honey Ant Readers: An innovative and bold approach to engaging rural Indigenous students in print literacy through accessible, culturally and linguistically appropriate resources." *Australian and International Journal of Rural Education* 24, no. 1: 79–89.

James, M. 2015a. *The Honey Ant Readers: teacher's book.* Alice Springs: Honey Ant Readers.

James, M. 2015b. Interview by Jasmin Peskoller. 19 August 2015. Audio.

King, N. and Horrocks, C. 2010. *Interviews in qualitative research.* London: SAGE.

Kramsch, C. 2009. "Cultural perspectives on language learning and teaching." In *Handbook of Foreign Language Communication and Learning,* edited by B. Seidlhofer and K. Knapp, 219–246. Boston/Berlin: Walter de Gruyter.

Ladson-Billings, G. 2017. "The (r)evolution will not be standardized: Teacher education, hip hop pedagogy, and culturally relevant pedagogy." In *Culturally Sustaining Pedagogies. Teaching and Learning for Justice in a Changing World* edited by D. Paris and H. S. Alim, 141–156. New York, NY: Teachers College Press.

Leitner, G. and Malcolm, I.G. 2007. "Introduction." In *Trends in linguistics: the habitat of Australia's Aboriginal languages: past, present, future,* edited by G. Leitner and I.G. Malcolm, 1–22. Berlin: Walter de Gruyter.

Lewthwaite, B.E., Boon, H.J., Webber, T., and Laffin, G. 2017. "Quality Teaching Practices as Reported by Aboriginal Parents, Students and their Teachers: Comparisons and Contrasts." *Australian Journal of Teacher Education* 42, no. 12: 80–97. http://dx.doi.org/10.14221/ajte.2017v42n12.5

Liddicoat, A.J. 2009. "Evolving ideologies of the intercultural in Australian multicultural and language education policy." *Journal of Multilingual and Multicultural Development* 30, no. 3: 189–203.

Lin, S., Williamson, F., Beetson, J., Bartlett, B., Boughton, B., and Taylor, R. 2021. "Quantifying low English literacy in Australian Aboriginal communities: a correlational study." *The Australian Educational Researcher* 48: 267–289. https://doi.org/10.1007/s13384-020-00388-7.

Lloyd, N.J., Lewthwaite, B.E., Osborne, B., and Boon, H. 2015. "Effective Teaching Practices for Aboriginal and Torres Strait Islander Students: A Review of the Literature." *Australian Journal of Teacher Education* 40, no. 11: 1–22. http://dx.doi.org/10.14221/ajte.2015v40n11.1

Lo Bianco, J. 2009. "Dilemmas of efficiency, identity and worldmindedness". In *Culturally and linguistically diverse classrooms: new dilemmas for teachers*, edited by J. Miller, A. Kostogriz, and M. Gearon, 113–131. Bristol, Multilingual Matters.

Lowe, K., Skrebneva, I., Burgess, C., Harrison, N., and Vass, G. 2020. "Towards an Australian model of culturally nourishing schooling." *Journal of Curriculum Studies*. https://doi.org/10.1080/00220272.2020.1764111.

Lowe, K., Tennent, C., Moodie, N., Guenther, J., and Burgess, C. 2021. "School-based Indigenous cultural programs and their impact on Australian Indigenous students: a systematic review." *Asia-Pacific Journal of Teacher Education* 49, no. 1: 78–98. https://doi.org/10.1080/1359866X.2020.1843137.

Malcolm, I.G. 2018. *Australian Aboriginal English: Change and Continuity in an Adopted Language*. Boston/Berlin: Walter de Gruyter.

Malcolm, I.G. and Sharifian, F. 2005. "Something old, something new, something borrowed, something blue: Australian Aboriginal students' schematic repertoire." *Journal of Multilingual and Multicultural Development* 26, no. 6: 512–532.

Malcolm, I.G. and Truscott, A. 2012. "English without shame: two-way Aboriginal classrooms in Australia". In *Rethinking education volume 5: harnessing linguistic variation to improve education,* edited by A. Yiakoumetti, 227–258. Bern, Peter Lang.

May, S. 2012. "Educational approaches to minorities: context, contest and opportunities". In *Rethinking education volume 5: harnessing linguistic variation to improve education,* edited by A. Yiakoumetti, 11–44. Bern, Peter Lang.

Mayring, P. 2015. *Qualitative Inhaltsanalyse: Grundlagen und Techniken*. 12th edn. Weinheim: Beltz.

McCandless, T., Fox, B., Moss, J., and Chandir, H. 2020. "Intercultural Understanding in the Australian Curriculum." *The Australian Educational Researcher* 47: 571–590. https://doi.org/10.1007/s13384-019-00358-8.

Milgate, G., and Giles-Browne, B. 2013. "Creating an Effective School for Aboriginal and Torres Strait Islander Students". Paper presented at the Annual Meeting of the American Educational Research Association (AERA), San Francisco, 2013. https://research.acer.edu.au/indigenous_education/32.

Moran, A. 2011. "Multiculturalism as nation-building in Australia: inclusive national identity and the embrace of diversity." *Ethnic and Racial Studies* 34, no. 12: 2153–2172.

Morisson, A., Rigney, L.-I., Hattam, R., and Diplock, A. 2019. *Toward an Australian Culturally Responsive Pedagogy. A narrative review of the literature.* University of South Australia.

NSW Department of Education 2020. "Aboriginal education policy". Last updated 09 June 2020. https://policies.education.nsw.gov.au/policy-library/policies/aboriginal-education-and-training-policy.

NSW Ministry of Health 2019. *Communicating Positively: A Guide to Appropriate Aboriginal Terminology.* Sydney: NSW Ministry of Health. https://www1.health.nsw.gov.au/pds/Pages/doc.aspx?dn=GL2019_008

Partington, G. 2003, 'Why indigenous issues are an essential component of teacher education programs', *Australian Journal of Teacher Education*, vol. 27, no. 2, pp. 39–48.

Partington, G. and Galloway, A. 2007. "Issues and policies in school education." In *Trends in linguistics: the habitat of Australia's Aboriginal languages: past, present, future* edited by G. Leitner and I.G. Malcolm, 237–266. Berlin: Walter de Gruyter.

Peltier, S. 2010. *Valuing children's storytelling from an Anishinaabe orality perspective.* Thesis. Nipissing University, Ontario. http://hdl.handle.net/1807/92898.

Peskoller, J. 2018. „Der multikulturelle Lernkontext indigener SchülerInnen in Australien – Herausforderungen und didaktisch-methodische Ansätze." In *ÖGSD Tagungsberichte Vol. 4/2018: Proceedings of the 10th ÖGSD Young Researchers' Conference,* edited by B. Fliri, 25–30. Graz: Österreichische Gesellschaft für Sprachendidaktik (ÖGSD).

Peskoller, J. 2019. "Essential Foundations. The Significance Of Aboriginal Australian Students' Home Language And Culture For Their Learning At School." In *Dritte „Tagung der Fachdidaktik" 2017 Religiöse und (sozio-)kulturelle Vielfalt in Fachdidaktik und Unterricht* edited by M. Juen, Z. Sejdini, M. H. Tuna, and M. Kraml, 195–210. Innsbruck: innsbruck university press.

Pike, M.A. 2015. *Ethical English: teaching and learning in English as spiritual, moral and religious education.* London: Bloomsbury.

Philips, J. and Luke, A. 2017. "Two Worlds Apart: Indigenous Community Perspectives and Non-Indigenous Teacher Perspectives on Australian Schools." In *Second International Handbook of Urban Education* edited by W.T. Pink and WG.W. Noblit, 959–996. Springer.

Power, T., Virdun, C., Sherwood, J., Parker, N., Van Balen, J., Gray, J., and Jackson, D. 2015. "REM: A Collaborative Framework for Building Indigenous Cultural Competence." *Journal of Transcultural Nursing* 27, no. 5: 439–446. http://dx.doi.org/10.1177/1043659615587589.

Ratcliffe, S. 2018. *Oxford Essential Quotations*. 6th edn. Oxford: Oxford University Press. http://dx.doi.org/10.1093/acref/9780191866692.001.0001.

Risager, K. 2018. *Representations of the world in language textbooks*. Bristol: Multilingual Matters.

Sarra, C. 2011. *Strong and Smart – towards a pedagogy for emancipation: education for first peoples*. Abingdon, Oxon: Routledge.

Sarra, C., Spillman, D., Jackson, C., Davis, J., and Bray, J. 2018. "High-Expectations Relationships: A Foundation for Enacting High Expectations in all Australian Schools." *The Australian Journal of Indigenous Education* 49, no. 1: 32–45. http://dx.doi.org/10.1017/jie.2018.10.

Seidman, I. 2013. *Interviewing as qualitative research: a guide for researchers in education and the social sciences*. 4th edn. New York: Teachers College Press.

Smith, H. 2008. "Biculturalism." In *Encyclopaedia of bilingual education* edited by J.M. González, 66–68. Thousand Oaks, CA: SAGE.

Stone, A., Walter, M., and Peacock, H. 2017. "Educational outcomes for Aboriginal school students in Tasmania: Is the achievement gap closing?" *Australian and International Journal of Rural Education* 27: no. 3: 90–110.

Stronger Smarter Institute 2017. *Implementing the Stronger Smarter Approach*. Stronger Smarter Institute Position Paper.

Surkamp, C. 2017. Metzler Lexikom Fremdsprachendidaktik. Ansätze – Methoden – Grundbegriffe. 2nd edn. Stuttgart: Springer.

Tedick, D.J., Christian, D., and Fortune, T.W. 2011. "The future of immersion education: an invitation to 'Dwell in Possibilty'." In *Immersion education: practices, policies, possibilities*, edited by D.J. Tedick, D. Christian, and T.W. Fortune, 1–10. Bristol: Multilingual Matters.

Thorpe, K., Burgess, C., and Egan, S. 2021. "Aboriginal Community-led Preservice Teacher Education: Learning from Country in the City." *Australian Journal of Teacher Education* 46, no. 1: 55–73. http://dx.doi.org/10.14221/ajte.202v46n1.4.

Throsby, D. 2001. *Economics and culture*. Cambridge: Cambridge University Press.

Trudgill, P. 2000. *Sociolinguistics: an introduction to language and society*. 4th edn. London: Penguin Books.

Vass, G. 2018. "'Aboriginal Learning Style' and Culturally Responsive Schooling: Entangled, Entangling, and the Possibilities of getting Disentangled." *Australian Journal of Teacher Education* 43, no. 8: 89–104.

Watkins, M., Lean, G., and Noble, G. 2016. "Multicultural education: the state of play from an Australian perspective." *Race Ethnicity and Education* 19, no. 1: 46–66. https://doi.org/10.1080/13613324.2015.1013929.

Williams, S. T. 2012. *The importance of teaching and learning Aboriginal languages and cultures: a mid-study impression paper.* Surry Hills, NSW: Aboriginal Affairs, Office of Communities NSW Government.

Windle, J. 2009. "Influences on the written expression of bilingual students: teacher beliefs and cultural dissonance." In *Culturally and linguistically diverse classrooms: new dilemmas for teachers* edited by J. Miller, A. Kostogriz, and M. Gearon, 92–109. Bristol: Multilingual Matters.

Wintergerst, A.C. and McVeigh, J. 2011. *Tips for teaching culture: practical approaches to intercultural communication.* White Plains, NY: Pearson.

Yiakoumetti, A. 2012. "Rethinking linguistic diversity in education." In *Rethinking education volume 5: harnessing linguistic variation to improve education,* edited by A. Yiakoumetti, 1–10. Bern, Peter Lang.

Yunkaporta, T. 2009, 'Aboriginal pedagogies at the cultural interface', PhD book, James Cook University, Townsville, viewed 25 November 2015, http://researchonline.jcu.edu.au/10974/.

Yunkaporta, T. 2010. "Our Ways of Learning in Aboriginal Languages." In *Re-Awakening Languages: Theory and practice in the revitalisation of Australia's Indigenous languages* edited by J. Hobson, K. Lowe, S. Poetsch, and M. Walsh, 37–49. Sydney: Sydney University Press.

Yunkaporta, T. 2020. *Sand talk. How indigenous thinking can save the world.* 1st edn. New York, NY: HarperOne.

Zubrick, S.R., Silburn, S.R., De Maio, J.A., Shepherd, C., Griffin, J.A., Dalby, R.B., Mitrou, F.G., Lawrence, D.M., Hayward, C., Pearson, G., Milroy, H., Milroy, J., and Cox, A. 2006, *The Western Australian Aboriginal child health survey: improving the educational experiences of Aboriginal children and young people.* Perth: Curtin University of Technology and Telethon Institute for Child Health Research.

Appendix: Interview Form

Name:_____   Position:_____

Location:_____

Date:_____   Start Time:_____

End Time:_____

INTRODUCTION

Hi, I am Jasmin Peskoller, lovely to meet you. Thank you for seeing me today — I really appreciate your support for my research project.

Due to your experience, you are an expert in the field of Indigenous education and teaching and learning with Indigenous students. Your participation in this study is meaningful and your information will contribute to research in the field of bilingual-bicultural teaching approaches with Indigenous students in Australia. After the conducted research, you will naturally be informed of its outcomes if you wish to be.

INTERVIEW

Part A: LANGUAGE

In this first part of the interview the focus is on language.

1. *In general terms, how does a student's home language influence his/her learning at school?*

   Possible follow-ups for all questions:

   Could you please clarify what you mean by …?
   Could you give an example?
   Could you describe this in more detail?
   Could you elaborate on that?

2. *How does an Indigenous Australian student's home language influence his/her English learning at school?*

3. *How does an Indigenous Australian student's home language influence his/her general learning at school?*

4. *Please rate the following on a scale from 1 to 10, 1 being "not important" and 10 being "very important".*

   How important is the consideration and incorporation of an Indigenous Australian student's home language in teaching materials and methodology for his/her English learning outcomes?

1	2	3	4	5	6	7	8	9	10

   Possible follow-up for the rating questions:

   You rated this as … (number). Could you expand/elaborate on that?

5. *Please rate the following on a scale from 1 to 10, 1 being "not important" and 10 being "very important".*

   "How important is the consideration and incorporation of an Indigenous Australian student's home language in teaching materials and methodology for his/her general learning outcomes?"

1	2	3	4	5	6	7	8	9	10

Possible follow-up for the rating questions:

You rated this as ... (number). Could you expand/elaborate on that?

6. How can Indigenous Australian students' home language be incorporated in teaching materials or methodology?

7. To what extent have you made adaptations or alterations in your teaching materials and ways of teaching?

Part B: CULTURE

The second part of the interview is about culture. Language, being a fundamental component of culture, has already been discussed separately in this interview.

8. In general terms, how does a student's home culture influence his/her learning at school?

   Possible follow-ups for all questions:

   Could you please clarify what you mean by ...?
   Could you give an example?
   Could you describe this in more detail?
   Could you elaborate on that?

9. How does an Indigenous Australian student's home culture influence his/her English learning at school?

10. How does an Indigenous Australian student's home culture influence his/her general learning at school?

11. Please rate the following on a scale from 1 to 10, 1 being "not important" and 10 being "very important".

    "How important is the consideration and incorporation of an Indigenous Australian student's home culture in teaching materials and methodology for his/her English learning outcomes?"

1	2	3	4	5	6	7	8	9	10

    Possible follow-up for the rating questions:

    You rated this as ... (number). Could you expand/elaborate on that?

12. *Please rate the following on a scale from 1 to 10, 1 being "not important" and 10 being "very important".*

    "How important is the consideration and incorporation of an Indigenous Australian student's home culture in teaching materials and methodology for his/her general learning outcomes?"

1	2	3	4	5	6	7	8	9	10

    Possible follow-up for the rating questions:

    You rated this as ... (number). Could you expand/elaborate on that?

13. *How can Indigenous Australian students' home culture be incorporated in teaching materials or methodology?*

14. *To what extent have you made adaptations or alterations in your teaching materials and ways of teaching?*

Part C: CHALLENGES

15. *What challenges exist in teaching and learning English with Indigenous Australian students?*

16. *What challenges exist in general teaching and learning with Indigenous Australian students?*

17. *Do you have any further comments/thoughts/ideas you would like to share?*

WINDUP

Thank you for supporting my research by participating in this interview. You will be informed about the outcomes of the research.

Painting her feet and stepping on a blank page during an open Art lesson at school at the age of 12, the author had no idea that the resulting painting would one day be the cover for her book on Indigenous Australian education.

ibidem.eu